Henry Sweetser Burrage

Rosier's Relation of Waymouth's voyage

to the coast of Maine, 1605

Henry Sweetser Burrage

Rosier's Relation of Waymouth's voyage
to the coast of Maine, 1605

ISBN/EAN: 9783744650601

Printed in Europe, USA, Canada, Australia, Japan

Cover: Foto ©ninafisch / pixelio.de

More available books at **www.hansebooks.com**

ROSIER'S RELATION

OF

WAYMOUTH'S VOYAGE

To the Coast of Maine, 1605,

WITH AN INTRODUCTION AND NOTES.

BY HENRY S. BURRAGE, D. D.

Printed for the GORGES SOCIETY, Portland, Maine.
1887.

CONTENTS.

I. INTRODUCTION, - - - - - 1
II. SURVEY OF THE LITERATURE, - - - 39
III. A TRVE RELATION, - - - - 76

ILLUSTRATIONS.

Portrait of Henry Wriothesley, Earl of Southampton,	Frontispiece.

FACING PAGE.

Autograph and Seal of Queen Elizabeth, - 20

Portrait of Thomas Arundell, Baron of Wardour, - - - - - 81

Monhegan as seen from the North, and the Camden Mountains as seen from Monhegan, - - 100

Chart of Coast from White Head to Pemaquid Point.

Chart of Coast from Pemaquid Point to Seguin Island.

PREFACE.

Rosier's "Trve Relation" has been reprinted in this country twice; once in the Collections of the Mass. Hist. Society, 3d Series, Vol. 8, (the copy for which was obtained in England by Jared Sparks), and again (a reprint of Sparks' copy) in a pamphlet published by George Prince, at Bath, Maine, in 1860. Original copies of the "Relation" are exceedingly scarce. Quaritch, the well-known London bookseller, has a copy which cost him at an auction sale not long ago £275, and for which he now asks £325. The John Carter Brown Library in Providence, R. I., secured a superb copy of this rare pamphlet several years ago. Through the kindness of Mr. John Nicholas Brown, I obtained permission in 1884 for a transcription of this original copy; and the work was performed by the Assistant Librarian of Brown University, Mr. John Milton Burnham, to whom I am greatly indebted for the painstaking service thus rendered.

vi PREFACE.

dered. It is his transcription of the original pamphlet that I have used in the present volume.

In the Introduction I have brought together such facts as I have been able to secure with reference to George Waymouth.

[signature: Geo: Waymouth]

Hitherto but little has been known concerning him. In my investigations I have been greatly aided by Mr. James P. Baxter, of Portland, who, during his residence in England in 1885 and 1886, left no place unvisited where there was likely to be found any trace of Waymouth's life and work. His labors were richly rewarded. Manuscripts were discovered which have remained unnoticed almost three centuries, and which throw much light upon the character and the career of one who has hitherto been known merely as a navigator. In the notes I have expressed my obligations to Mr. Baxter for the materials which he generously placed at my disposal. I am also indebted to him for valuable suggestions concerning difficult points that have presented themselves in the course of my work.

I exceedingly

PREFACE.

I exceedingly regret that even with Mr. Baxter's enthusiastic aid I have been unable to discover the time and place of Waymouth's birth and death. It has been intimated that the late Henry Stevens, a resident of London, with whom Waymouth was a favorite subject for study, possessed facts concerning Waymouth's life which had eluded the search of others. But the recent publication of the Court Minutes of the East India Company from 1599 to 1603,* prepared by Mr. Stevens, and published by his son, Mr. Henry N. Stevens, leads me to believe that not much is to be expected from this source. In these records is preserved the action of the Company with reference to Waymouth's voyage in 1602 in search of a north-west passage to the Indies: and one would suppose that either in the introduction, or in the notes printed in connection with the record, at least some of the facts which had been gathered concerning Waymouth would be inserted. But for any such facts one will search this volume in vain. The omission is almost as notable as would be the absence of any reference to Waymouth's life in a reprint of Rosier's "Relation."

In

---

*The Dawn of British Trade to the East Indies, as Recorded in the Court Minutes of the East India Company, 1599-1603, containing an account of the formation of the Company, the first adventure and Waymouth's Voyage in search of the North-West Passage, now first printed from the original manuscript by Henry Stevens, of Vermont. With an introduction by Sir George Birdwood, Kt. London, Henry Stevens & Son, 1886.

In his preface, however, Mr. Henry N. Stevens expresses the hope that some interesting particulars respecting Waymouth may yet be gleaned from memoranda made by his father.

The name of Waymouth's vessel is not given by Rosier; nor is it found in the accounts of the voyage recorded by Strachey, Purchas or Gorges. Prince (Me. Hist. Soc. Coll., Vol. 6, p. 294) says that Waymouth's ship is "supposed to have been called the Archangel." So far as I can ascertain, living somewhat remote from large libraries, the name of the vessel first appears in Dr. John Harris's Collection of Voyages and Travels, p. 223, Vol. II., Revised Edition, London, 1748. The first edition appeared in 1702-5. John Harris, D. D., (1667-1719) was one of the early members of the Royal Society, and for a while acted as its Vice President.

In preparing the "Survey of the Literature," I endeavored carefully to examine all the references in published volumes to points in controversy connected with Waymouth's voyage in 1605. It did not occur to me, however, to include in my search "The Revised Statutes of the State of Maine." In this I erred, for Hon. C. W. Goddard, by whom the revision was made, has an introductory chapter on the "Sources of the Land Titles of Maine," and in a note on page VI., he says:

"Although

PREFACE.

"Although any further contributions toward a solution of the long vexed question of the identity of Waymouth's explorations may seem superfluous, the commissioner, after a personal examination of those waters in a sail-boat in August, 1882, ventures to express his concurrence in the opinion of Captain George Prince, of Bath, first published in 1858, that Pentecost Harbor was probably George's Island Harbor, and not Boothbay; that the very high mountains which might be discovered a great way up in the main, could not possibly have been the White Mountains, or any other than the Camden Hills; and that the great river trending alongst into the main towards the great mountains, which Strachey, (not Waymouth, or Rosier, Waymouth's companion and historian) calls 'that most excellent and benefycial river of Sagadahoc,' but which Sir Ferdinando Gorges calls the 'Pemaquid,' must have been the George's and not the Kennebec or the Penobscot."

If this testimony had come under my notice earlier it would have been included in my "Survey of the Literature."

In my work, aside from the persons already mentioned, I have received valuable assistance from Dr. C. E. Banks, of the U. S. Marine Hospital Service. Many notes which he had prepared with reference to Waymouth's voyage

x   PREFACE.

voyage of 1605 he kindly placed in my hands. I am indebted to him, also, for the use of his excellent etching of Thomas Arundell, Baron of Wardour, after a photograph of a portrait in the possession of the Arundell family. At my request, too, he has made for this work two additional etchings, one of Monhegan Island from the North, after a sketch on one of the Coast Survey charts, and another of the Camden Mountains as seen from Monhegan, after a drawing which I made near the school-house on Monhegan in the summer of 1885.

To the United States Coast and Geodetic Survey Office, Washington, D. C., I am indebted for the two excellent charts which will be found in a pocket at the close of the volume. One of these charts, showing the coast from White Head to Pemaquid Point, includes also Monhegan, St. George's Island Harbor and the St. George's River; the other, the coast from Pemaquid Point to Seguin Island. A line in red ink on the first chart indicates the probable course Waymouth took after leaving his anchorage north of Monhegan, in entering Pentecost Harbor, and afterwards in sailing up the great river he discovered. A like line indicates, so far as this chart is concerned, the course he followed, if we identify Pentecost Harbor with Fisherman's Island Harbor or Boothbay Harbor. Lines in red ink on the
                                                          second

PREFACE.

second chart are used to indicate Waymouth's course if he entered the Kennebec at Bath by way of Townsend Gut, Sheepscot Bay and the Sasanoa River, as Sewall and others suppose, or if he sailed up the Kennebec from its mouth, as is maintained by Ballard and others. These lines in red ink, which were added by William S. Edwards, first assistant city civil engineer, Portland, cannot but be helpful to the readers of the following pages.

My grateful acknowledgments for helpful suggestions, are also due to Prof. James Bryce, of Oxford University, England, and to Prof. Asa Gray, of Harvard University; and especially to the Secretary of the Maine Historical Society, Mr. Hubbard W. Bryant.

HENRY SWEETSER BURRAGE.

Portland, Me., Feb. 1, 1887.

INTRODUCTION.

IN the latter part of the sixteenth century, several attempts were made to plant English colonies in North America. The first of these attempts was made by Sir Humphrey Gilbert,[1] who had been knighted in 1570, for distinguished military services in Ireland. In 1578, having obtained an extensive grant of land in the northern part of North America, he sailed from England with his half-brother, Sir Walter Raleigh;[2] but on account of various disasters which

---

1. For more than twenty years, by petitions, and at length by an elaborate treatise, Gilbert had urged upon Elizabeth and her ministers the importance of western discovery and colonization. He was the second son of Otho Gilbert, and his mother, whose maiden name was Catherine Champernown, married, after her husband's death, Walter Raleigh, and by him had two sons, Carew and Walter. At the time of Walter's birth, Humphrey Gilbert was thirteen years of age.

2. "He lived in the County of Devon, bordering easterly upon the sea, and saw the ships depart for the new found lands, and, when they returned, heard the stories of the captain and sailor, of the wonders they

which befel the expedition, he was compelled to return without having set foot on the shores of the new world.

Four years later, in 1583, with five ships and two hundred and sixty men, Gilbert (Raleigh being detained at Court by the Queen, who did not wish her favorite to be exposed to "dangerous sea-fights,") again left England for the land beyond the sea, and this time succeeded in reaching Newfoundland, of which he took possession in the name of Queen Elizabeth. On the return voyage, Sept. 9, 1583, his vessel, of ten tons burden only, too heavily laden, foundered, and Gilbert with all on board perished.[3]

In the following year, April, 27, 1584, Sir Walter Raleigh,

had witnessed and the exploits they had performed. In his boyhood, he read the tales of Spanish discovery, conquest and possession in the new world, and conceived a youthful admiration for the heroism in danger, and fortitude and patience in suffering, which he had occasion enough to remember in his own subsequent fortunes, and which he expressed in the review of his life from the outlook of the Tower, in his History of the World." Dr. Leonard Woods, in the introduction to the Documentary History of the State of Maine, Vol. 2, p. xlii. Concerning Raleigh, see a well prepared memoir by Rev. Increase N. Tarbox, D. D., in "Sir Walter Ralegh and his Colony in America." Prince Society, Boston, 1884.

3. Only two vessels, the "Squirrel" and the "Golden Hind," remained of the fleet that left England. Sir Humphrey was on the "Squirrel." Hayes, Captain of the Golden Hind, reports: "On Monday, the 9th of September, the frigate [the 'Squirrel'] was near cast away, yet at that time recovered; and giving forth signs of joy, the general, sitting abaft with a book in his hand, cried out to us in the 'Hind,' 'We are as near to heaven by sea as by land.'" That night the frigate foundered.

Raleigh, who after Gilbert's death had been made lord proprietor of a large tract of territory in the new world —his patent, almost identical in terms with that of Gilbert, was dated March 25, 1584,[4]—despatched thither two vessels under the command of Philip Amidas and Arthur Barlow. On reaching the American coast, they explored Pamlico and Albemarle Sounds, and on their return to England they reported their discoveries in such glowing language that the interest of the Queen was enlisted, and she gave to the newly discovered territory the name Virginia.

In 1585, having received added favors from the Queen to assist him in his work of foreign discovery, Raleigh fitted out another expedition consisting of seven vessels, with one hundred and eight emigrants, under the command of Sir Richard Grenville. A settlement was made at Roanoke Island, and Grenville returned to England with the ships, leaving Ralph Lane in command of the colony: but in the following year, when reinforcements reached Roanoke Island, it was found that the colony had been abandoned, and that Sir Francis Drake, who was

---

4. Strachey [Historie of Travaile into Virginia, Hakluyt Soc., Reprint, p. 8,] says it was "a large graunt, from 33 to 40 degrees of latitude, exemplified with many ymmunityes and priviledges." The patent is in Hazard's State Papers, pp. 33-38, also in "Sir Walter Ralegh and his Colony in America," pp. 95-105, Prince Society, 1884.

was on the American coast that season, had picked up Lane and his companions, and sailed for England.[5]

In 1587, Raleigh made an added attempt to plant a colony in the new world. A site farther north, on the shores of Chesapeake Bay, was selected by him; and a large body of emigrants, who should become the founders of an agricultural State, were sent thither under command of John White, who left England April 27th, with a charter of incorporation for the "city of Raleigh." But the colonists landed on Roanoke Island, in site of the former settlement. Two vessels with supplies were subsequently sent to them by Raleigh, but were so crippled by Spanish cruisers that they were obliged to return

---

5. "Sayling along by a wasted coast, they found certaine *Englishmen* which had settled themselves in Virginia, so named in honour of Queene ELIZABETH, a Virgin, whom Sir Walter Raghley, a man in great favour with *Queene* ELIZABETH, had sent thither of late for a colony in a most commendable desire to discourer farre countries, and to advance the glory of *England* for nauigation. To *Ralph Lane*, their captaine, *Drake* offered all offices of kindness, and a ship or two with victuals, and some men, if he thought good to stay there and prosecute his enterprise; if not, to bring them back into England. But whilest they were lading of victuals into those ships, an extraordinary storme carried them away, and dispersed the fleet in such sort, that they met not again till they came into *England*. Hereupon *Lane* and those which were carried thither, being in great penury, and out of all hope of victuals out of *England*, and greatly weakened in their number, with one voyce besought *Drake* that he would carry them back again to their owne country, which hee willingly did." History of the Reign of Elizabeth, by William Camden, London, 1685, pp 285, 286.

turn to England, and the colonists, overtaken by "a miserable and untymely destiny," perished. Having exhausted all of his means, Raleigh made no further attempts to colonize his possessions in North America, and when the seventeenth century opened not a single Englishman was to be found at any point on the coast from Newfoundland to Florida.[6]

But notwithstanding the failure of the various enterprises with which Raleigh was connected, there were those in England to whom the colonization of some part of the American coast was still a cherished dream. Newfoundland at that time was visited annually by a large fishing fleet, "about four hundred sails of ships,"[7] as an old document states. But Newfoundland was "a cold and intemperate place, not to be traded nor frequented at all times, nor fortified for security of the ships and goods: oft spoiled by pirates or men of war: the charges great for salt, double manning and double victualling their ships, in regard that the labor is great and the time long, before their lading can be ready; they carry outwards

---

6. Though Raleigh's Virginia enterprise failed, "his hopes were strong enough to withstand the failure of nine several expeditions, and the natural discouragement of twelve years' imprisonment. Just on the eve of his own fall from outward greatness, he had written, 'I shall yet live to see it an ENGLISH NATION. That faith remained with him to the Tower, and he did live to see his prediction realized." Edwards' Life of Raleigh, Vol. 1, p. 91.

7. Coll. Mass. Hist. Soc., 3d Series Vol. 8, p. 98.

6 ROSIER'S RELATION.

outwards no commodities for freight; and after six months' voyage, their return is made but of fish and oils." If farther south, therefore, in a more temperate and agreeable climate, a flourishing colony could be established, there would be a demand for the products of the mother country, and a great and constantly growing trade would thus be established. It was from motives like these that a few enterprising Englishmen at the opening of the seventeenth century turned their thoughts toward these western shores.

The first effort in the seventeenth century to plant an English colony in North America, was made by Captain Bartholomew Gosnold,[8] who sailed from Falmouth, England, March 25, 1602, in a small bark called "The Concord." He was accompanied by thirty-two persons, eight of whom were mariners. Of the entire number, twelve purposed to return to England " upon the

8. Gosnold was an experienced mariner, and had been employed in one of the earlier expeditions to the American coast. Belknap [Am. Biography, 2, p. 101,] says, " At whose expense he undertook the voyage to the northern part of Virginia does not appear." But Strachey, Historie of Travaile into Virginia [Hakluyt Society, reprint, p. 153] says: "A great and right noble earle amongst us,

'Candidus et talos a vertice pulcher ad imos,'
Henry, Earle of Southampton," largely contributed to the fitting out of this expedition. He also states that at the same time, Sir Walter Raleigh fitted out a vessel which he despatched, in 1602, to Virginia, under the command of Samuel Mace, " to fynd out those people which he had sent last thither by Capt. White, in 1587."

WAYMOUTH'S VOYAGE, 1605.

the discovery," and the rest were to remain "for population." The point Gosnold aimed to reach was "the north part of Virginia," the somewhat indefinite tract of territory granted to Raleigh by the Queen; and he made land north of Massachusetts Bay, not far from a point which he called "Savage Rock," because "the savages first showed themselves there." Sailing southward along the coast, he passed Cape Cod, which received this name from Gosnold because of the "great store of codfish" he there secured, and at length came to an island which he called Martha's Vineyard, and which Archer describes as "full of wood, vines, gooseberry bushes, whortleberries, raspberries, eglantines," &c. Here also he "took great store of cod, as before at Cape Cod, but much better." Sailing in toward the main land, Gosnold came to an island which he called Elizabeth's Isle, now Cuttyhunk;[9] and here he made preparations

---

[9] "To this spot I went on the 20th day of June, 1797, in company with several gentlemen whose curiosity and obliging kindness induced them to accompany me. The protecting hand of Nature has reserved this favorite spot to herself. Its fertility and its productions are exactly the same as in Gosnold's time, excepting the wood, of which there is none. Every species of what he calls 'rubbish,' with strawberries, pease, tansey and other fruits and herbs, appear in rich abundance, unmolested by any animal but aquatic birds. We had the supreme satisfaction to find the cellar of Gosnold's storehouse, the stores of which were evidently taken from the neighboring beach." Dr. Jeremy Belknap, Am. Biog., Vol. 2, p. 220. Harper's Ed.

preparations for a settlement. A store-house and a small fort were erected. But when Gosnold had loaded his small vessel with sassafras,[10] cedar, fur and other commodities, which he had obtained for the most part by traffic with the Indians, and was ready to return to England, some of the company who had "vowed to stay" refused so to do, and "the planters diminishing," the settlement was reluctantly abandoned. Gosnold, who on his return voyage sailed Friday, June 18, reached England, Friday, July 23."

The accounts of this voyage, one by Gabriel Archer, and the other by John Brereton, both of whom accompanied

---

10. "Sassafras, a plant of souereigne vertue for the French Poxe, and as some of late have learnedly written, good against the Plague and many other Maladies." Pring, in Mag. of Am. History, Vol. 8, p. 843. "The powder of sassafras in twelve hours cured one of our company that had taken a great surfeit, by eating the bellies of dog fish, a very delicious meat." Archer's Relation of Gosnold's Voyage, Mass. Hist. Coll., 3d Series, Vol. 8, pp. 77, 78. "The sassafras tree is no great tree. I have met with some as big as my middle: the rind is tawny and upon that a thin colour of ashes, the inner part is white, of an excellent smell like Fennel, of a sweet taste with some bitterness: the leaves are like fig leaves, of a dark green." Josselyn's Two Voyages to New England Boston, 1865, p. 55.

11. In 1607, Gosnold, with Capt. John Smith, led to Virginia a colony which settled at Jamestown. There, not long after his arrival, Gosnold died. In George Percy's account of the first settlement of Virginia occurs this note: "The 22d of August died Captain Bartholomew Gosnold, one of our council. He was honorably buried, having all the ordnance in the fort shot off, with many volleys of small shot. After his death the Council could hardly agree." Purchas his Pilgrimmes, iv, p. 1690.

panied Gosnold, were published in England after the expedition returned. In glowing language their "Relations" depicted the magnificence and fertility of the country, compared with which, said Brereton, the most fertile part of England was but barren. And he adds: "We stood awhile like men ravished at the beauty and delicacy of this sweet soil; for besides divers clear lakes of fresh water (whereof we saw no end), meadows very large and full of green grass; even the most woody places (I speak only of such as I saw) do grow so distinct and apart, one tree from another, upon green, grassy ground, somewhat higher than the plains, as if nature would show herself above her power, artificial."[12] Archer said: "This main is the goodliest continent that we ever saw, promising more by far than we any way did expect, for it is replenished with fair fields, and in them fragrant flowers, also meadows, and hedged in with stately groves, being furnished also with pleasant brooks, and beautiful with two main rivers that (as we judge) may haply become good harbors, and conduct us to the hopes men so greedily do thirst after."[13]

Especially in the seaport towns the publication of these "Relations" awakened added interest in the new world.

12. Brereton's "Relation," Mass. Hist. Coll., 3d Series, Vol. 8, p. 89.

13. Mass. Hist. Coll., 3d Series, Vol. 8, p. 78.

world. "Sundry of the chiefest merchants of Bristol,"[4] to whom Master Richard Hakluyt,[5] Prebendary of St. Augustine's Cathedral Church, presented "many profitable and reasonable inducements," resolved to undertake further discoveries. Having first secured the permission of Sir Walter Raleigh, a recognition which Gosnold unhappily had overlooked as he found on his return, they fitted out two vessels, the Speedwell of about fifty tons, and the Discoverer of about twenty-six tons, with Martin Pring as "Master and Chiefe Commander." Sailing from Milford Haven, April 10, 1603, Pring took a direct course for the "North Coast of Virginia," which he sighted in latitude 43½°, on an unknown day in June, and passing along the coast of Maine, probably from Penobscot Bay, he "beheld very goodly groues and woods, replenished with tall okes, beeches, pine trees, firre trees, hasels, witchhasels and maples. We saw here, also, sundry sorts of beasts, as stags, deere, beares, wolues, foxes, lusernes and dogges with sharp noses." But finding no sassafras, Pring shaped his course for Savage Rock, "discouered

14. It was from this port that Sebastian Cabot in 1497 made his voyage to America.

15. This was the well known author of "The Principal Navigations, Voyages and Discoveries made by English Natives." He was appointed prebendary of Bristol in 1584 [Documentary History of the State of Maine, Vol. 2, p. xxxviii, note]: and of Westminster in 1605. He died Oct. 23, 1616, and was buried in Westminster Abbey.

"discouered the yeere before by Captaine Gosnold." Here also he found no sassafras, and he "bare into that greate Gulfe [Massachusetts Bay] which Captaine Gosnold ouer-shot the yeere before, coasting and finding people on the North side thereof. Not yet satisfied in our expectation, we left them and sailed ouer, and came to Anchor on the South side, in the latitude of 41 degrees and odde minutes; where we went on Land in a certain Bay, which we called *Whitson Bay*, by the name of the Worshipfull Master *John Whitson*, then Maior of the Citie of *Bristoll*, and one of the chiefe Adventurers, and finding a pleasant Hill thereunto adioyning, wee called it *Mount Aldworth*, for Master *Robert Aldworth's* sake, a chiefe furtherer of the Voyage, as well with his Purse as with his Trauell. Here we had a sufficient quantitye of Sassafras."[16]

Bancroft and Palfrey, following Belknap, identify Whitson's Bay with the harbor of Edgartown, Martha's Vineyard, which is in the latitude of 41°; 25'. The language of Pring's narrative, however, seems to indicate that he passed from the north to the south side of the "greate Gulfe," and Dr. B. F. DeCosta,[17] more accurately, perhaps, identifies Whitson's Bay with Plymouth Harbor, and "the pleasant Hill adioyning" with "Captain's Hill, or,

16. Mag. of Am. Hist., Vol. 8, p. 841.
17. Mag. of Am. Hist., Vol. 8, pp. 808, 809.

or, possibly, Manomet." The Discoverer was loaded with sassafras and despatched to England at the close of July. About the 9th of August, Pring followed in the Speedwell, and arrived in England October 2.[18]

> 18. There is a monument to Pring in St. Stephen's Church, Bristol, England, with this inscription:
>
> TO THE PIOUS
> MEMORIE OF MARTIN PRINGE,
> MERCHANT, SOMETYME GENERALL TO THE
> FRATERNITY OF THE
> TRINITIE HOUSE.
>
> The living worth of this dead man was such,
> That this fay'r Touch can give you but A Touch
> Of his admired guifts; Theise quarter'd Arts
> Enrich'd his knowledge and ye spheare imparts;
> His heart's true embleme where pure thoughts did moue;
> By a most sacred Influence from aboue,
> Prudence and fortitude are topp this tombe,
> Which in brave Pringe tooke up ye chiefest roome;
> Hope—Time supporters showe that he did clyme,
> The highest pitch of hope though not of tyme.
> His painefull, skillful trauayles reacht as farre,
> As from the Arctick to the Antarctick starre;
> Hee made himselfe A Shipp, Religion
> His onely compass, and the truth alone
> His guiding Cynosure, faith was his salles,
> His anchour hope, A hope that never failes;
> His freighte was charitie, and his returne
> A fruitfull practise. In this fatal vine
> His shipp's fayr Bulck is lodg'd, but ye ritch ladinge
> Is housed in heaven never fadinge.
>
> Obit Anno { Salutatis, 1626.
>   { Ætatis,   46.
>
> This monument was Beautified by Mrs. Hannah Oliver, Widdow, 1733. Mag. of Am. Hist., Vol. 9, p. 211.

Pring's safe return, and the reports which he brought of the fertility of the country and of the prospect of trade with the Indians, (which in 1604, with the French in Canada, in beaver and otter skins alone, amounted to thirty thousand crowns), confirmed the report of Gosnold, and increased the interest that had already been awakened in the new world beyond the seas.

Among those who had aided in fitting out Gosnold's expedition was Henry Wriothesley, Earl of Southampton, the well known English statesman to whom Shakespeare, in 1593, dedicated his "Venus and Adonis." He was connected with Essex in the conspiracy to seize the person of Elizabeth, and though on his trial he protested that he had never entertained a thought against the Queen, he was stripped of his titles and estates and thrown into prison. In the first year of James I., however, he was released from confinement, and his titles and estates were restored to him by a new patent July 21, 1603. Shortly after occurred the return of Pring, and, in his ardor for new enterprises, where could he find so inviting a field for noble endeavor as in the land beyond the seas, concerning which Pring, confirming Gosnold, had brought such favorable reports? Moreover, by reason of the changed fortunes of Raleigh,[19] the lands across

10. Dr. Leonard Woods, in his introduction to Vol. 2, of the Documentary History of Maine, p. xlvi, says that Raleigh held this grant un-

across the Atlantic, of which he had been lord proprietor for so many years, had now reverted to the crown, and wise management might secure the prize that so suddenly had fallen from Sir Walter's grasp. Accordingly, in the year 1604, he planned a new voyage of discovery. Associated with him were his son-in-law, Thomas Arundel, afterwards Baron of Wardour,[20] and Sir Ferdinando

til its forfeiture by the attainder of James in 1603. This seems to be based upon a statement in Strachey's introduction to his Historie of Travalle into Virginia [Hakluyt Society reprint, p. 0]: "which, true yt is, before Sir W. R. his attaynder, without his leave we might not make intrusion uppon, the title being only in him." Raleigh was arrested in the summer of 1603 on the charge (of which he is now believed to have been guiltless) of having conspired with others " to deprive the king of his crown and dignity, to subvert the government and alter the true religion established in England, and to levy war against the king." He was tried before Chief Justice Popham, and having been found guilty was by him sentenced to death. Dec. 15, 1603, while he was preparing to lay his head upon the block, a reprieve came from the king, and he was transferred to the Tower, where he remained until March 20, 1616, except for a brief period, during the plague, in which he was confined in the Fleet Prison because of the unhealthiness of the Tower.

20. Thomas Arundell, Baron of Wardour, was the oldest son of Sir Mathew Arundell, Kt., whose father, Sir Thomas Arundell, married Margaret, daughter of Edward Howard, third son of Thomas, Duke of Norfolk, and sister to Queen Catherine. He served as a volunteer in the imperial army in Hungary, and having in an engagement with the Turks near Strigonium taken their standard with his own hand, he was created by Rudolph II., Emperor of Germany, a count of the Empire by patent, dated Prague, Dec. 14, 1595. He was elevated to the peerage, as Baron Arundell, of Wardour, May 4, 1605. He died Nov. 7, 1639, at Wardour Castle, and was buried at Tysbury. His first wife was Mary, daughter of Henry Wriothesley, Earl of Southampton. His second wife was Ann, daughter of Miles Philipson, of Crook, County of Westmore-

Ferdinando Gorges,[21] whose name is thenceforward so prominent in the history of the colonization of this part of the American coast.

The command of this new expedition was given to Captain George Waymouth, a native of Devonshire,[22] probably of one of its seaport towns. He had a good English education, and for many years continued his studies in mathematics, especially in geometry. He became also an accomplished draughtsman. His studies, however, must have been continued after he entered upon a sea-faring life, inasmuch as he had to do with ships, as he tells us, as soon as he was able to do anything,

---

land. Dr. C. E. Banks, of the U. S. Marine Service, has a valuable genealogical table of "the noble family of Arundell Baron Arundell of Wardour"; also an old engraving by Fittler of a painting by R. Smirke, representing Sir Thomas Arundell taking the standard of the Turks.

21. This appears in a letter written by Sir Ferdinando Gorges, dated Plymouth, March 13, 1607, and addressed to "Mr. Challinge"—Capt. Henry Challoung, who in 1606 was placed by Gorges and others in command of an expedition to the American coast which proved a failure. Referring to Challoung's venture, Gorges says: "You know that the journey hath bene noe smale chardge to us, yt first sent to the coast, and had for our returne but the five saluages," *i. e.*, the five Indians captured by Waymouth, of whom Gorges, on Waymouth's return to England, received three. As Sir John Popham received the remaining two of these Indians, it is possible that he also had an interest in the voyage.

22. Narratives of Voyages towards the Northwest. Publication of the Hakluyt Society, London, 1849, p. 238. The place where Waymouth was born I have been unable to ascertain, although an extended search was instituted. James P. Baxter, Esq., when in England in 1885–6, aided me greatly in this investigation, but his usual good fortune failed him in this instance.

anything, and served "in well neere four prentize shipps," passing through all grades of the service, and filling "all the offices belonging to this trade, even from the lowest unto the highest." He extended his studies beyond the art of navigation, and made himself familiar with ship-building and also with the art of fortification.

We have no record of any of his voyages until 1602, when, under the patronage of "the Worshipful Fellowship of the Merchants of London trading into the East Indies," he made a voyage in search of a Northwest passage to the Indies. The proposal for such an undertaking was brought to the notice of the Fellowship, July 24, 1601. On that day, a letter, "written by one GEORGE WAYMOUTH, a navigat[r], touching an attempte to be made for the discovery of the Northwest passage to the Est Indies," was laid before the General Court. After deliberation, the matter was postponed to another meeting, which was held August 7, and at which it was voted to engage in such an expedition. Waymouth entered the service of the Fellowship in September. May 2, 1602, having made his preparations for the voyage, he sailed from the Thames with two vessels, the Discovery and the Godspeed, bearing with him the following letter from Queen Elizabeth to the Emperor of Cathay:

"Elizabeth,

"Elizabeth, by the Grace of God Queen of England, France and Ireland, Defender of the faith, &c., To the great, mighty and Invincible Emperour of Cathaia, greeting. Wee haue receiued dyuers and sondry relacons both by our owne subiects, and by others, whoe haue uisited some parts of your Ma^{ts} Empire and Dominions, whereby strangers that resorte unto yor Kingdomes with trade of merchandize wch hath wrought in vs a desire to fynde oute some neere waye of passage by seas from vs into your countrey, than the vsuall frequented course that hetherto hath byn houlden by compassing the greatest part of the world: By which neerer passage, not only opportunity of entercourse of traffique of merchandize may be offred betweene ye subiects of both o^r Kingdomes, but also a mutuall league and amity may growe, and be contynued, betweene yor ma^{tie} and vs, o^r Cuntries and Dominions being in their distance of scituacons not so farr remote, or seuered, as they are estranged and vnknown the one to the other, by reason of the long and tedious course of Navigacon hetherto vsed from theis parts unto you: To which ende wee haue heretofore many yeares past and at sundry tymes synce, made choice of some of o^r subiects, being a people by nature enclyned to great attempts, and to the discouery of contries and Kingdomes vnknowen, and sett

them

them in hand wth the fynding out of some neerer passage by seas into yor Ma^ts contries, through the North or East parts of the world, wherein hetherto not preuayling, but some of their ships neuer returning back agayne, nor being heard of synce their departure hence, and some of them retourning back agayne being hindered in their entended voyage by the frozen seas, and intollerable cold of those clymates: Wee haue yett once more, of o^r earnest desire to try the vttermost y^t may be done to p forme at length a neerer discovery of yor Contrye, prepared and sett fourth two small shipps vnder ye deriction of our subiect and seruant George Waymouth, being ye principall Pylott of this present voyage, a man for his knowledge and experience in nauigacon specially chosen by vs to this attempte, whom if it shall please God so to prosper in his passage, y^t either hee or any of his company aryue in any part of your Kingdome, wee pray yor Matie in fauo^r of vs, who haue soe desired ye attayning this meanes of accesse vnto yo^u, and in regard of an enterprize p formed by hym and his company, wth so great difficulty and danger, y^t you will vse them wth that regard y^t may gyve them encouragem^t to make this their newe discouered passage, wch hetherto hath not byn frequented or knowne by any to become a vsuall frequented trade from this pte of ye world to y^r Matie. " By

"By which Meanes yor contrey may hereafter be serued wth the natyue comodityes of theis parts of speciall seruice and use, both for yor Matie and subiects may be furnished wth thinges of lyke seruice and vse; out of wch mutuall benefitt, amity and frendshipe may growe and be established betweene vs wch wee for o^r part will not lett hereby to offer vnto you for the honorable report wch wee haue heard of yor Matie. And because in y^{is} first discouery of the waye to yor contrey, it seemed to vs not convenient to ymploy shipps of that burthen wch might bring in them any great quantity of o^r natyue comodityes whereby they might be pestered wee did resolue to vse small shipps as fittest for an vnknowen passage, laden for ye most part wth such necessaries as were of vse for their discouery; it may please yor Matie by the pticulers of such things as are brought in theis shipps, to vnderstand yt of goods of those kyndes o^r kingdome is able to furnish yor Matie most amply, and also of sundry other kynds of merchandize of like vse, where of it may please yor Matie to be more pticularly enformed by the said George Waymouth, and his company, of all wch upon significacon vnto vs by yor Ma^{ts} Lres to be returned by o^r said subiect, yt our uisiting of yor kingdomes w$_{th}$ our shipps and merchandize shall be acceptable and kyndly receiued, we will in the next fleet

w^{ch}

wch we shall send vnto you make it more fully appeare what vse and benefitt o^r amity and entercourse may bring to yor Matie and contrey. And in the meane tyme do commend yor Matie to the protection of eternall God, whose prouidence guideth and pserveth all Kinges and Kingdomes. From our Royall Pallace of Greenwiche the fourth of May an° dni 1602 and of o^r Raigne 44".

(Superscribed) " To the Right High mighty and Invincible Emperor of Cathayc."[23]

On the 18th of June Waymouth sighted the southern part of Greenland, bearing north about ten leagues. A course more or less westerly was then followed until June 28, when land was discovered, which was at first supposed to be the American coast, but which proved to be Cape Warwick, or Earl Warwick's Foreland, to the northward of Resolution Island. July 8th, land was again discovered, but on account of the ice the vessels could

---

23. The original copy of this letter, written upon vellum, with a highly illuminated border upon a red ground, and signed at the bottom by Queen Elizabeth in her largest sized hand, was found in London about a half century ago, in tearing away an old closet, in a house where repairs were in progress. The letter was accompanied by separate translations on paper in Italian, Latin and Portuguese. Jan 28, 1841, Sir Henry Ellis, by the kindness of Mr. Hogarth, of Portland St., laid this letter before the Society of Antiquaries, in London; and the letter, with fac-simile of the signature of the Queen and also of the seal attached (of a type not before engraved), was printed in their proceedings. The original letter has disappeared. For this curious document, and its history, I am indebted to James P. Baxter, Esq.

Queen Elizabeth's signature and seal attached to the letter which she sent by Waymouth.

could not approach it. The cold was now intense. "When the men came to hand them they found the sayles, ropes, and tacklings so hard frozen, that it did seem very strange, being in the cheefest time of summer." Waymouth persevered, however, in his endeavor to overcome the obstacles in his way. But at length a mutiny broke out; and he was reluctantly compelled to return to England. He arrived in Dartmouth Harbor Aug. 5, 1602, a few days after Gosnold's return from Elizabeth Island. A narrative of the voyage was laid before the "Worshipful Fellowship of Merchants," Sept. 16. The failure of the expedition was evidently keenly felt by all the members of the company, and an investigation of the causes that led to the failure was at once instituted. Waymouth was examined not only by the Court of Committees of the East India Fellowship, but by the Lords of the Privy Council. He seems to have cleared himself of all blame in the matter, and it was decided that "being very competent," he should have command of a second expedition. This second expedition was the subject of prolonged discussion at the meetings of the company from Nov. 24, 1602, to May 24, 1603, and was then for a time abandoned, apparently from pecuniary considerations. Waymouth's connection with the Fellowship now probably came to an end, and he was ready to embark in any other enterprise that offered. His

His experience as a navigator, and his skill in other directions, deserved, as he believed, recognition from the King, and in order to bring himself to the favorable notice of his royal master, James I., he prepared a work on navigation, ship-building, &c., entitled "The Jewell of Artes."[24] In his dedication to the King, referring to his work, Waymouth says:

"I undertooke the same for the wealth of youre majestie my soueraine lorde and King and of your highnesse realmes and Dominions minding to haue published it for the good of this whole comon wealth: but considering with my selfe that if I shoulde comitt it to the presse, the coppies thereof might be conueyed home and so foraine nations, for whome I nothing meant it should reape as much proffit of it as this my natiue cuntrie I therefore of dutie present the same to youre royall majestie, referring the publishing of the whole booke or any parte there of only to youre majestie's high prudence and discretion. the other that youre highnesse a most wise and gratious prince hauinge duely considered these my laboures and in them my good intent, would

---

[24] This manuscript James P. Baxter, Esq., of Portland, Me., discovered in 1885 in the King's Library, in the British Museum, London. On account of the light which it throws upon Waymouth's character and career, he caused a *fac simile* copy to be prepared, which is now in his possession. For the use of this copy and other manuscripts, references to which will appear later, I am indebted to him.

would vouchsafe to give sentence of me whether I may be able to Deserue maintenance and imployment at home, or for my necessarie releese enforced to seeke the same a broade in foraine cuntries : for all though in the performance here of I have so farre neglected my necessarie affaires as I am all to gether unable any longer to supporte my meane estate. yett shall your highnesse but vouchsafe to affirme me worthie of preferment at home in this youre famous Kingdome I shall thinke my trauell herein fullie rewarded, be it only with youre fauourable acceptance of the same which in all humblenesse of Dutie I freely give unto Royall Majestie and in it my whole state and this with all my selfe, to be orderd at your highnesse princelie Discretion, most humblie beseeching youre highnesse to accept the same as the worke of youre poore subject that daylie indeauoreth to imploy that still that god hath lent him to the increasment of the wellfeare of youre royall majestie and to the benefett of this youre famous monarchie being most desirous to make due proofe unto youre highnesse of all things Demonstrated in this present booke when so euer it shall please youre highnesse to command me."

"The Jewell of Artes," thus laid before the King, is a manuscript volume of three hundred and twenty pages, elegantly

elegantly bound, the covers emblazoned with the royal arms and sprinkled with lions rampant.

The work is divided into seven books, as follows:

1 In the first where of as well the auntient instrument of nauigation newly corrected and most plainely described by Demonstratiue figures, as other more exact not before knowne

2 In the seconde the manner of building shippes by a geometricall proportion both shewing the faultes here tofore comitted in building and howe to a voyde them, and allso howe to make them more offensiue and defensiue than those nowe used

3 In the thirde the manner, of making of Enjines for diuerse uses most comodious both for sea and lande newly inuented

4 In the foureth how to take height of, any tower castle or other building with the demonstrations of the most necessarie instrumentes to suruey lande with, and, allso a most exact instrument for the inlargeing or reducing of any lande keeping allwayes the selfe same shape

5 In the fift diuerse most comodious plattes fore fortification sett forth by plaine demonstrations with a most exact instrument shewing the manner howe to direct a mine to any object, and to knowe whether the
                                                                    enimes

enimes doe countermine with Diuerse other deuises to offend him, and to Defend the place beseiged in most excellent manner

6 In the sixte the manner of making the most seruiceable kinde of ordinance that ever was Deuised and the most artificall cariages for the same being nimble and easie to remoue by menes of an Engine there unto added

7 In the seauenth the excellentist instruments for gunners arte that euer were deuised with many most plaine Demonstrations howe A gunner ought to place his ordinance to batter any object all which conclusions are to be wrought by the practise of Arithmeticke and geometrie without the which no man can attaine to any perfect knowledg in those artes. where unto is added A breefe table for the findeing of the square and cubique seruing to many right Excellent uses.

In the preface Waymouth states at some length the reasons why he was unsuccessful in his voyage for the discovery of the North-west passage. The following are some of the " Demonstrations " with which the work abounds:

"The Demonstration of the astrolabe to take the height or altitude of the sunne by her shadowe."

The

"The Demonstration of a most exacte astrolabe to take the altitude of the sunne whose Degrees are larger then any yet used, and will serue both at sea and lande."

"The Demonstration of A most excellent Instrument to finde the height of the pole and the true hower all times of the day if the Sunne geve any shadowe, the place of the sume and the variation of the needle being first knowne all those partes on both sides are partes beloingen the this instrument."

"The Demonstration of a most exact compasse seruing most excellent to finde the variation of the needle and allso to Direct a shippe by."

"The Demonstration of a compasse without a needle seruing to direct a shipp by the shadowe of the sunne and by the helpe of a watch when other compasses with the needle are out of use."

"The Demonstration of an Instrument to finde the tydes in all places, the flowing or the change of the moone being first knowen." "The manner of making an equinoctiall Diale. A example when you be to the southe ward of the equinoctiall and the sunne hauen south Declination howe to finde the height of the pole."

"How to finde the height of the pole by the meridianall height of the sunne and her declination without finding the height of the Equinoctiall." Among

Among other drawings is one of an engine, by which a ship may be defended from a multitude of men assaulting the same with "pikes swords or small shot": Waymouth says:

"This Engine ought to be made rounde A foote or 15 inches heigh from the superficies of the thing where upon it is to be placed in the circumference where of ought to be placed 6 or 8 small murdering peeces which will carry some 40 or 50 muskett bulletes A peece and betweene euery 2 of those murderers must allso be placed one blad of Iron and steele made verry sharpe as well upon both edges as allso on the pointe being stronglie fastened in to the same the whole Engine being couered over with boardes verry close and hauing in the very dest of it A winch of Iron to turne it About to any corner or part of the shipp where in it shall be Assaulted the men that use it being close couered under it out of sight and danger may so feircely and speedely discharge the saide peeces in to any one or diuerse partes of a shipp where it is Assaulted as they may soone Destroy the enemie and preserue them selves there shipp and goodes from being taken as Aboue said and if this Engine shoulde suddenly be forced uppon by great multitud of people yet might it be so violentlie turned about by those that are under it that

that no man might endure to lay hand uppon it but that those blades woulde euen chopp them in peeces you may with this Engine hauing but 10 or 12 men to use the same defend a shipp from being taken by 3 hundred yea if I were to builde a shipp my self after a proportion that I could prescribe (god assisting me with out whose blessing all policies are of no force) I would so contriue the same as if it were but of one hundred tunne and hauing only but 20 men in it by meanes of this Engine I would defend the same from being taken by fiue hundred men useing only the weapons Aboue rehearsed. The Demonstration of this Engine you may see plainely Demonstrated."

In the fourth book we are told:

"How to measure the height of A tower at 2 stations."
"To measure the deepnesse of any well."
"To take the distance from any platform bullworkes or such like yf the gunners be of good skill in this parte and then hee shall not meese his marke that hee shoote at or ther ways he may which would be A shame unto the gunner and A increasement of the enemys Joye."
"The Demonstration of a Instrument to take the height with of any wall or castle the use where of is shewed in this booke by A geometricall table."

The

The chapter on fortifications contains many excellent and elaborate drawings, some beautifully colored.

One " Demonstration showeth howe by a whole circle to line out a fort, castle or towne in forme of a triangle," another " in forme of a quadrant angle," another " in form of a cinqu angle," and another " in forme of a sextile angle." There is a " Demonstration of the foundation and bullwarkes of a castle whose Ditches are Defended by there vaultes, and allso the Demonstration of the same castle standing upright, and the skale to measure euery parte there of." Also the " Demonstration of the foundation and bullwarkes of a castle whose Ditches are Defended by there flanckes," with many illustrations. A " Demonstration howe to be siege a towne and howe the towne beseiged may Defend it selfe, all whose bullwarkes are built circular." A " Demonstration of a castle beseiged on 3 sides with a scale to measure ther distance betweene the castle and those that Doth beseige the same." Then follow directions " howe to guide any kinde of mine, leuel or not to wardes any towne or castle or other object and to knowe when yee are come derectly under that place and howe much yee ar under the same and how to guide any mine enclining upward or downward directly upon any point Assigned allso the manner yf you shoulde by the way be
inforced

inforced by water or workes or any other impedementes, howe you may carrie the mine upon any other pointe or degree what so euer from the direct coourse and howe you shall all ways knowe still the certaine place where you are and howe farre yee are distante from the first entire of the mine and like wise the distance from the place yee desire to goe."

In the seventh book are given "demonstrations of diuerse most necessarie Instrumentes for gunners arte neuer yett knowne." The drawings are exceedingly elaborate and finely executed.

"The Jewell of Artes" bears no date, but this mention of the voyage of 1602, as of recent occurrence, and the silence of the work concerning the voyage of 1605, enable us to assign it to the year 1603 or 1604. James I. was proclaimed King on the death of Queen Elizabeth, March 24, 1603, but he did not reach London until about the middle of April. As "The Jewell of Artes" contains about two hundred pages of drawings, many of them exceedingly elaborate and in several colors, Waymouth could hardly have placed it in the King's hands earlier than the beginning of 1604.

The work must have made on the King and those about him an impression exceedingly favorable to its author. But it failed to bring employment in the royal service

service as Waymouth evidently hoped. I like to think, however, that the labor he had spent in its preparation was not altogether in vain. Certainly it is possible that among those who were permitted to turn its pages, and look upon its beautiful and elaborate "Demonstrations," was the Earl of Southampton; and that in part, at least, it was Waymouth's skill as a navigator, as illustrated in "The Jewell of Artes," that led to his appointment as commander of the vessel in which he visited the coast of Maine in 1605.

It is the account of this voyage, and the important discoveries made in connection with it, that Rosier gives in his "Relation."

The success of this voyage of 1605 brought Waymouth into public notice, but it did not secure for him what he so much desired—employment in the royal service. One book in his "Jewell of Artes" is devoted to a consideration of defects in ship-building, and the way in which to remedy these defects. His views on this subject he now again[25] put forth in a brief paper entitled "Errors and Defects in vsuall building of Ships," a manuscript copy of which, though not in Waymouth's handwriting, is in the British Museum. In it occurs this reference to himself: "My

---

25. The manuscript has no date, but it contains more points than the book on this subject in "The Jewell of Artes," and seems best to belong to this period of Waymouth's life.

"My study this twenty yeares in ye Mathematicks hath been cheefly directed to ye mending of these defects. I have during this tyme applied my self to know ye sevrall wayes of building, & ye secrets of ye best shipwrightes in England & Christendome; and haue lykewise observed ye workings of ships in ye sea in all ye voyages I have been. By these helps I have demonstratively gayned ye science of making of ships perfect in Art, which of necessity must be wrought by a differing way from all ye shipwrights in ye world."

Though Waymouth failed to obtain employment from the King, his services were at length acknowledged. By Privy Seal dated Oct. 27, 1607, and Patent dated Nov. 11, 1607, a pension of three shillings and four pence per day was granted to him. The record in the Public Records Office in London is as follows:

"Georgio Waymouth, gentili, de annuitate sua ad iii s. iiii d. per diem solvenda durante vita sua, ad quatuor anni terminos, per litteras Domini Regis Patentes dates XI die Novembri Anno Regni sue Auge. etc quinto . . . Habendum a festo sancti Michaelis, archangeli, ultimo preterito, ei debito pro dimidio anni finito ad festum Annuntiationis pred —— xxx li, viii s. iiii d."

The first payment to Waymouth, as the Issue Rolls show, was made May 11, 1608.   Not

WAYMOUTH'S VOYAGE, 1605.

Not long after, Waymouth became involved in an unpleasant controversy. On account of complaints made to the King, a royal commission was appointed to investigate certain abuses in the public service, the alleged purpose being the "Reformation and saveing of great sums to his majestie which he expended yearly in the maintenance of his ships." Phineas Pette,[26] a master shipwright, who at that time was engaged in building a "great ship" for the King, at Woolwich, refers in his "Journal" to the investigations made by this commission with reference to his own work. From his account, it appears that Waymouth was employed by the commission as an expert. Referring to his opponents, Pette says:

"They had alsoe wonne to their Partie by much importunity and by means of a particular letter directed from the Lord Northampton to him to that very purpose

---

26. Phineas Pette was the son of Peter Pette, of Deptford, one of her Majesty's shipwrights, and was born Nov. 1, 1570. In 1586, he was sent to Emmanuel College, Cambridge. His father died in 1589, and in the following year, for lack of means, he was unable to continue his residence at Cambridge, and was apprenticed to a shipwright at Deptford. Further misfortunes came to him; but at length better days returned, and in time he attained to eminence as a shipwright. This manuscript "Journal," which records his varying fortunes, and is of interest on account of his public service and the glimpses it gives us of King James I., the Prince, and other prominent persons, is in the British Museum. A copy, containing 321 pages, is in the possession of James P. Baxter, Esq., Portland, Me.

pose a great Bragadochio a vage and idle fellow some time a Mariner and M^r called by the name of Captaine George Waymouth who having much acquaintance abroad amongst gentlemen was to disperse the insufficiency of my business reporting how I was no Artist and altogether insufficient to Performe such a service, of noe experience," etc.

At the hearing before the King, Pette's opponents failed to substantiate the charges they had brought against him, and he was acquitted by the King. Pette, who can hardly find words with which to express his contempt for Waymouth, and gleefully narrates a case in which the latter's failure as a shipwright is sketched, says that early in November, 1609, Waymouth humbly apologized to him for the part he had borne in the accusations made to the King.

The next we hear of Waymouth is in connection with the siege of Julich, an important town in one of the Rhine provinces, and about sixteen miles northeast of Aix-la-Chapelle. A dispute had arisen in 1609, on the death of the Duke, John William, with reference to the Julich succession. The Duke died childless, and it was seen that if the territory which he had ruled should fall into the hands of the Roman Catholics, the hopes of the States would be crushed. If, on the contrary, it should

should fall into Protestant hands, the States would be greatly strengthened. And so Prince Maurice marched upon Julich in the summer of 1610, and, with other forces which were added to his, laid siege to the place and captured it. This was the beginning of the Thirty Years' War.

Our knowledge of Waymouth's connection with this siege is derived from a manuscript in the King's Library in the British Museum. It is entitled "A Journall Relation of the service at the takeing in of the towne and castle of Gulicke this present yeare 1610, with a plott of the towne and castle as it is againe to be fortified. George Waymouth."[27] The manuscript gives a detailed account of the siege, the names of the officers in command, and the three places where battles were fought, to which is added a plan of the fortification. It is possible that during this siege Waymouth had an opportunity of testing some of his own speculations with reference to military operations.

Nothing

---

27. This manuscript, like the two other Waymouth manuscripts to which I have referred, was discovered by James P. Baxter, Esq. It bears upon the cover the royal arms, with the initials G. II. R. 1757, showing that the manuscript belonged to George the Second. It is in the same handwriting as the manuscript on "Errors and Defects in usuall building of Ships." The manuscript is not signed or dated. "The name George Waymouth," says Mr. Baxter, "is in the hand of the scribe and has a line drawn through it. It was neatly written, but contains many erasures and corrections, probably suggested by Waymouth after hearing it read."

Nothing further concerning Waymouth is known except in connection with the payment of his pension. The last entry which can be found is on the Issue Roll for Easter, 1612, at which date Waymouth was still alive. There are unfortunately no existing rolls for Michaelmas, 1611, Easter, 1612, or Easter, 1613, and as the name of Waymouth does not appear on the intermediate rolls, viz: those for Easter, 1611, Michaelmas, 1612, and Michaelmas, 1613, nor in those of the following years, 1614–1616, it may be presumed that the last payment made to him was either at Michaelmas, 1612, Easter, 1613, or Easter, 1614, which payment would in all probability precede or follow his death.

Waymouth's writings show that he was a man of more than ordinary intelligence in all matters pertaining to his profession. As Mr. Baxter says: " He was no rough mariner, as we have heretofore supposed, but a scholar, a dreamer indeed, like Raleigh, of whom he reminds me, especially in his treatise on ships, which was also a theme of Raleigh's pen." He must have had, however, some important defects of character or his advancement could hardly have been prevented. His end doubtless brought to him a glad release. With the exception of his voyage of 1605, ill fortune attended him for the most part. Disappointment followed disappointment, and death

death in all probability robbed him of no coveted honor.

Concerning Rosier, I have been able to learn no more than what appears in his "Relation." Belknap (Am. Biography, Harper's Ed., Vol. 2, p. 208, note) says that Rosier was connected with Gosnold's expedition, and wrote an account of the voyage, which he presented to Sir Walter Raleigh. This is an error made by Purchas, who in his "Pilgrimmes" (IV. pp., 1646–1653) cites three documents relating to Gosnold's voyage to America in 1602: 1. A letter from Capt. Gosnold to his father; 2. Gabriel Archer's account of the voyage; 3. A chapter entitled "Notes taken out of a tractate written by James Rosier to Sir Walter Raleigh." This tractate presented to Raleigh was not written by Rosier, but by John Brereton.[28]

It has been said that in his "Relation," Rosier wrote obscurely so that enterprising navigators in other countries might not profit by Waymouth's discoveries. This is true so far as locality is concerned. There were those in these countries who, as he says in his prefatory note to the reader, "hoped hereby to gaine some knowledge of the place." And he adds: "This is the cause that I haue neither written of the latitude or variation most exactly obserued by our Captaine with sundrie instruments

---

28. Gosnold's letter to his father, and Archer's and Brereton's narratives are in Mass. Hist. Col., 3d Series, Vol. 8.

struments, which together with his perfect Geographicall Map of the countrey, he entendeth hereafter to set forth."[29] He likewise omitted a collection of many Indian words, reserving them "to be made knowen for the benefit of those that shal goe in the next Voyage." But this was all that was withheld. "Our particular proceedings in the whole Discouerie," he says, "the commodious situation of the Riuer, the fertilitie of the land, with the profits there to be had, and here reported, I refer to be verified by the whole Company, as being eyewitnesses of my words." Rosier could hardly have used stronger language in insisting upon the absolute accuracy and trustworthiness of his narrative.

29. Rosier, near the close of his "Relation," again refers to this purpose. Waymouth unquestionably made a report, which included, as is here stated, a carefully prepared map; but neither the report nor the map can now be found.

SURVEY OF THE LITERATURE.

REFERENCES to Waymouth's voyage are to be found in the narratives of subsequent navigators, in histories, and other writings. The following citations are from the more important of these references.

Champlain was on the coast of Maine in 1605, as was Waymouth. From his narrative (Voyages of Sieur de Champlain, published in Paris in 1613, Prince Society Ed., Vol. 2, pp. 55–93) we learn that he left the island of St. Croix June 18 (N. S.) 1605. Following the coast as far as Cape Cod, he reached the Kennebec on his return July 29. From an Indian named Anasou he then learned:

"That there was a ship, ten leagues off the harbor, which was engaged in fishing and that those on her had killed

killed[30] five savages of this river[31] under cover of friendship. From his description of the men on the vessel we concluded that they were English, and we named the island[32] where they were La Nef; for at a distance it had the appearance of a ship."

The next reference to Waymouth's voyage is found in a "Relation of a Voyage into New England, begun from the Lizard ye First of June 1607, by Captⁿ Popham in ye Ship ye Gift, and Captⁿ Gilbert in ye Mary and John," written, it is thought, by James Davies, one of the Council of the Popham Colony, who accompanied the expedition.[33] Of the two vessels mentioned, the

---

30. As will be seen in the ".Relation" this was an error. The savages were made captives at Pentecost Harbor, and were taken to England.

31. In the words "of this river" Slafter, (Champlain's Voyages, Prince Society Ed., Vol. 2, p. 91) finds an intimation that the river discovered by Waymouth was the Kennebec. If, however, Waymouth had been in the Kennebec with his ship, Anasou could hardly have failed to mention it. What he doubtless meant was that the Indians captured by Waymouth belonged to the tribe to which he belonged. This tribe occupied the territory between the Kennebec and the Penobscot. That the captives were Pemaquid Indians is evident for reasons that will be given in connection with Rosier's account of their capture.

32. This island, as all writers agree, so far as I am aware, was Monhegan, and it is worthy of notice that Anasou locates Waymouth's ship so far away from the Kennebec. It is evident that he had received only rumors in reference to Waymouth, and those, too, of not a very recent date, as Waymouth had sailed for England several weeks before.

33. The manuscript of this sketch was found in the summer of 1875, in the Library of Lambeth Palace, London, by the Rev. B. F. DeCosta, D. D., of New York. "A sort of title page," he says, "has been prefixed to the manuscript, in an early hand, by a former possessor, reciting that it was

the first to arrive on the coast was the Mary and John. August 6th, having sighted the Camden Hills—"three high mountains that lie in upon the mainland near unto the river of Penobscot, in which river the bashabe makes his abode,"—Capt. Gilbert stood in toward them until noon. Changing his course then to the west, he sighted three islands "lying together, being low and flat by the water, showing white as if it were sand, but it is white rocks making show afar off almost like unto Dover Cliffs." They were Seal, Wooden Ball and Ragged Islands of the Matinicus group, which "lie due east and west one of the other." The narrative continues:

"From hence we kept still our course west and west by north towards three other islands that we saw lying from these islands before spoken of eight leagues, and about ten of the clock at night we recovered them, and having sent in our boat before night to view it, for that it was calm, and to sound it and to see what good anchoring was under it, we bore in with one of them, the which

found among the papers of Sir Ferdinando Gorges by one William Griffith." Dr. De Costa obtained permission to copy the manuscript for publication, and in May, 1860, he laid his copy with a preface and notes before the Massachusetts Historical Society. His communication is printed in the Proceedings of the Society, Vol. 18, pp. 82-117. A comparison of the narrative with chapters VIII, IX, and X., of "Strachey's Historie of Traualle Into Virginia Britannia" showed that either that manuscript, or a copy of it, was used by Strachey in his preparation of his work, as "portions of the manuscript were copied by him almost verbatim."

which as we came in by we still sounded, and found very deep water forty fathom hard aboard of it. So we stood into a cove in it, and had twelve fathom water, and there we anchored until the morning, and when the day appeared we saw we were environed round about with islands; you might have told near thirty islands round about us from aboard our ship. This island we call St. Georges Island,[34] for that we here found a cross set

---

[34]. Dr. De Costa (Proceedings Mass. Hist. Soc., Vol. 18, p. 101, note) is of the opinion that the island near which Capt. Gilbert anchored was Monhegan. But Monhegan cannot be reached on a "west and west by north" course from Capt. Gilbert's position approaching the Matinicus Islands. Furthermore, on such a course, Monhegan would not appear as one of three islands, but an island by itself. Nor would one at anchor under Monhegan find himself "environed round about with islands." There is not an island, except Manana, within five nautical miles. As Rev. Henry O. Thayer, in a paper read before the Maine Historical Society, Dec. 22, 1885, referring to this point, says: "This is a clearly impossible statement applied to Monhegan. The nearest neighbors to the lonely Isle are Allen's and Burnt, six miles distant. Still further away on the left, a practiced eye in fine weather can make out three or four small ones stretching towards Pemaquid. In the clearest atmosphere, Seguin in the west, and in the east, Matinicus and Metinic, perhaps another, can be distinguished at those long distances. An ordinary observer would at first notice only two,—Allen's and Burnt; with a sharper eye sweeping the horizon one might count nine or ten. But their distance makes this language wholly forced and inadmissible. Even the two of the Georges at their distance would never be referred to as environing a ship. The description is entirely inapt in application to Monhegan." The St. Georges Islands, on the other hand, are eight leagues distant from the Matinicus Islands, and in the direction mentioned. In St. George's Harbor, too, one could very properly say that he was "environed round about with islands." There are more than thirty islands in a radius of ten miles.

set up, the which we suppose was set up by George Wayman."³⁵

The Gift, Captain Gilbert's consort, came to the same anchorage on the following day, which indicates a previous agreement on the part of the commander of his vessels. In other words here was the chosen rendezvous.³⁶ The narrative continues:

"This night following about midnight, Captain Gilbert caused his ship's boat to be manned and took to himself thirteen other, myself being one, being fourteen persons in all, and took the Indian Skidwarres with us. The weather being fair and the wind calm, we rowed to the west in amongst many gallant islands, and found the river of Pemaquyd to be but four leagues west from the island

---

35. The finding of this cross is significant. In Rosier's "Relation" we read that on the 29th of May, 1605, Waymouth, while his vessel was at anchor in Pentecost Harbor, "set up a cross on the shore side upon the rocks." Gilbert undoubtedly had a copy of Rosier's "Relation" with him, and was evidently looking for this cross, else why not mention Pring who was on the coast in the preceding year, or Champlain, or Gosnold, who preceded Waymouth?

36. This statement is confirmed by Sir Ferdinando Gorges in his Briefe Narration (Maine Hist. Soc. Collections, Vol. 2, p. 21), where it is remarked, "They arrived at their rendezvous the 8th of August." Rev. Henry O. Thayer adds: "There was evidently a design to tarry at this place,—a politic and honorable one,—to make early acquaintance with and gain the favor of the natives. Skidwarres, returning with them after his knowledge of the world across the sea, acted as guide, interpreter and assistant in this bit of diplomacy and incipient statecraft, as the representatives of the British throne and possessions of choice chartered rights, sought friendly alliance with a native tribe in the new world."

island we call St. Georges, where our ship remained still at anchor. Here we landed in a little cove by Skidwarres direction, and marched over a neck of land near three miles. So the Skidwarres brought us to the savages houses where they did inhabit, although much against his will, for that he told us that they were all removed and gone from the place they were wont to inhabit; but we answered him again that we would not return back until such time as we had spoken with some of them. At length he brought us where they did inhabit, where we found near a hundred of them, men, women and children, and the chief commander of them is Nahanada."[37]

The next reference to Waymouth's voyage is in Captain John Smith's Description of New England, which was published in London in 1616. Capt. Smith was on the coast of Maine in the summer of 1614. In his

---

[37]. Nahanada was one of the Indians captured by Waymouth in 1605. He must have returned with Pring in his voyage of 1606. Skidwarres was also one of Waymouth's captives. It is supposed by some that Captain Gilbert, under the guidance of Skidwarres, proceeding in his boat westward, passed Pemaquid Point, and thence made his way to Pemaquid Harbor. He certainly did, if by rowing he found what is now known as Pemaquid River. The distance from St. George's Harbor to Pemaquid Harbor is about the same as that mentioned, viz: four leagues. But from the fact that after landing, Gilbert and his party "marched over a neck of land near three miles," seems rather to indicate that they landed at New Harbor and crossed the Neck to Partridge's Point, where they found the Indian camp and also "the river of Pemaquyd."

his Description (Veazie Reprint, Boston, 1865, p. 22,) he says:

"Northward six or seven degrees is the Riuer *Sagadahock*, where was planted the Westerne Colony, by that Honourable Patrone of vertue Sir John Popham Lord Chief Iustice of England.[38] Ther is also a relation printed by Captaine *Bartholomew Gosnould*, of Elizabeth's Iles: and an other by Captaine Waymoth of Pemmaquid."[39]

In

38. The fact that the Popham Colony settled at the mouth of the Kennebec has been urged in favor of the theory that the river discovered by Waymouth was the Kennebec. It is to be remembered, however, that Pring was on the coast in 1606, in the interest of the same parties as Waymouth in the preceding year, and on his return, having made "a more perfect discovery of *all* those rivers and harbors," laid before Gorges his "most exact discovery of that country." Those familiar with the history of the voyage of the Popham colonists will remember that as the vessels proceeded westward from the place of *rendezvous*, the landmark they looked for was Seguin. "Thursday in the morning, break of day, being the 13th August, the Island of Sutquin bore north of us, not past half a league from us, and it riseth in this form hereunder following [a sketch is given], the which island lieth right before the mouth of the river Sagadehock south from it neer two leagues, but we did not make it to be Sutquin, so we set our sails and stood to be westward for to seek it two leagues further, and not finding the river of Sagadehock, we knew that we had overshot the place." (Proceedings Mass. Hist. Soc., Vol. 18, p. 103.) Rosier makes no mention of this striking landmark, and such knowledge must have been received from Pring. Prince, in his pamphlet on "Rosier's Narrative," also suggests that a good and sufficient reason why the Popham colonists settled at the mouth of the Kennebec was, "that the French laid claim to and were at this time colonizing at the eastward, and it was considered desirable to locate as far from their rivals as convenient."

39. If Waymouth printed a "Re-

46   ROSIER'S RELATION.

In Smith's Generall Historie of Virginia (Book 1. p. 18, sq.) published in London in 1626, there is a condensed account of Rosier's narrative of Waymouth's voyage. After referring to the island (Monhegan) where Waymouth first landed, Smith says:

"From hence we might discerne the mayne land and very high mountaines, the next day because we rode too open to the Sea, we waighed, and came to the Isles adioining to the mayn; among which we found an excellent rode, defended from all windes, for ships of any burthen in 6, 7, 8, 9 or 10 fadom vpon a clay oze. This was vpon a Whitsonday, wherefore we called it *Pentecost Harbour.*"[40]

Between the publication of Smith's Description of New England and his Generall Historie of Virginia, William Strachey wrote, probably in 1618, his Historie of Travaile into Virginia Britannia. In chapter vii. (Maine Hist. Soc. Collections, Vol. 3, p. 287) he gives an account of "Capt. George Weymouth's voyage." He says:

"What lation" it has not been preserved. In all probability, Smith has in mind Rosier's "Relation," which he used in preparing his Generall Historie. The fact worthy of notice here is that by Pemaquid, Smith evidently meant a place, not a river. He also knew Pemaquid from Sagadahoc. In his narrative he correctly locates the Popham Colony on the Kennebec, but he fails anywhere to connect Waymouth with that river.

40. As Smith professes to give only a condensation of Rosier's "Relation," it is not necessary that I should quote further.

"What paines he tooke in discovery may witness the many convenyent places upon the mayne, and isles, and rivers, together with that little one of Pamaquid," and of

41. As Strachey had Rosier's "Relation" before him when he wrote, the reference here evidently is to the "little narrow nooke of a riuer" up which the Indians endeavored to lure Waymouth and his men for the purpose of trade, as they claimed, but with hostile designs as Waymouth feared. That this "little narrow nooke of a riuer" was what is now known as the Pemaquid River, as is commonly taken for granted, is merely an inference. The references to the Pemaquid River in early documents that have come down to us show that, in most cases certainly, what is now known as the Pemaquid River could not have been in the minds of those who used this designation in their writings. Thus in 1025 Purchas (His Pilgrimmes, Vol. 4, p. 1673), giving the names of the rivers in the country of Mawooshen, mentions the Pemaquid, which he says is "four days journey [sixteen miles, as the estimate shows] from the mouth of the Quibiquesson, with ten fathoms of water at the mouth, and forty miles up the river there were two fathoms and a half at low water; on both sides of this river for a good distance, the ground is like unto a pleasant meadow, full of long grass."

This certainly could not be what is now known as the Pemaquid River.

In the letters patent to Robert Aldworth and Giles Elbridge, of Bristol, under the seal of the President and Council of New England, dated Feb. 29, 1631, signed by the Earl of Warwick and Sir Ferdinando Gorges, there is a grant of 12,000 acres, "the same land to be bounded, chosen, taken and laid out neare the River Comonly called or known by the name of PEMAQUID, or by what other name or names the same is or have been or hereafter shal be called or knowne by and next adioyning by both along the Sea Coast as the Coast lyeth; and Soe upp the River as farr as may Containe the said Twelve Thousand acres within the said bredth and length." (Col. Me. Hist. Soc., Vol. 5, p. 210.) The implication is that the 12,000 acres might be laid out "upp the River" without reaching its source; but no one would use such language in laying out such a tract of land on what is now known as the Pemaquid River.

The members of the Plymouth Council, in 1635, determined to surrender their charter to the King on condition that the territory which it included should be granted to them-

of his search sixty miles up the most excellent and beneficyall river of Sagadehoc, which he found capable of shippinge for trafique of the greatest burden, a benefitt, indeed,

selves. They proposed to divide the territory into twelve Royal Provinces. The first (Williamson, Hist. of Maine, Vol. 1, p. 256) "embraced the country between the St. Croix and Pemaquid, and from the head of the latter in the shortest distance to Kennebec, thence upward to its source." The second Province included the territory from "Pemaquid to Sagadehock." Plainly the reference here is not to what is now known as the Pemaquid River.

The next reference to the Pemaquid River which I find is in Maverick's Description of New England, written probably in 1660. He says: "Westward from Penobscott (which is the Southermost Fort in Noua Scotia) fourteen Leagues of is Pemaquid in which River Alderman Aldworth of Bristole, setled a company of People in the yeare 1625, which Plantation hath continued and many Families are now settled there." (New Eng. Hist. and Gen. Register, Vol. 39, p. 34.) This settlement of 1625 was made on the eastern side of the Neck, and the reference to the river must be to some other than what is now known as the Pemaquid River.

In the grant to the Duke of York, dated March 12, 1664, occurs the following: "Charles the Second by the Grace of God King of England, Scotland ffrance & Ireland Defender of the ffaith &c To all to whom these p'nts shall come Greeting: Know yee that wee for diverse good Causes and Consideracons us thereunto moving Have of our speciall Grace Certaine knowledge and meere motion Given and Granted And by these presents for us our heires and successors Do Give and Grant unto our Dearest Brother James Duke of Yorke his heires and Assignes All that part of the Maine Land of New England beginning at a Certaine place called or knowne by the name of St. Croix, next adjoyning to New Scotland in America and from thence extending along the sea-coast unto a certaine place called Petuaquine or Pemaquid and so up the River thereof to the farthest head of ye same as it tendeth northwards and extending from thence to the River Kinebequi, and so upwards by the shortest course to the River Canada northwards." (Coll. Me. Hist. Soc., Vol. 5, pp. 6 and 7 of Pemaquid Papers.) The western boundary here is evidently the same as that of the first of the "Royal Provinces," which the members of the Plymouth Council carved out for

indeed, alwais to be accompted the richest treasure to any land."[42]

In Purchas His Pilgrimmes (Vol. 4, p. 1660,) printed in London in 1625, Rosier's "Relation" appears in an abridged form, but with a few additions. In the most important of these we have the direction of the high mountains seen by Waymouth from his anchorage north of Monhegan. The passage is as follows:

"From themselves; but no one would have thought of making what is now known as the Pemaquid River such a boundary.

In the commission of Major Edmund Andros, as Governor of New York, which was dated July 1, 1674, we read: "James Duke of Yorke and Albany, Earl of Ulster, &c Whereas it hath pleased ye King's most Excellent Ma^{ts} my Soveraigne Lord and brother by his Lett^{rs} Patents to give and grant unto mee and my heyres and assignes all that part of ye Maine Land of New England beginning at a certaine place called or knowne by ye name of St. Croix next adjoyneing to New Scotland in America, and from thence extending along ye sea Coast unto a certaine place called Pemaquin or Pemaquid and soe up the River thereof to ye furthest head of the same as it tendeth northwards and extending from thence to the River Kinebequi and soe upwards by ye shortest course

to ye River Canada northwards," &c. (Documents relating to Colon. Hist. of New York, Vol. 3, p. 215.) The language here is similar to that already cited.

42. By the river of "Sagadehoc" Strachey means the Kennebec. But it should be remembered that Strachey was never on the coast of Maine. He came to Virginia in 1609, and was for a time secretary of the colony, but returned to England before 1612, and wrote the "Historie," it is supposed, about 1618. His information, therefore, was second hand. That Rosier's "Relation" was before him as he wrote his account sufficiently indicates. He also had before him, as has already been remarked, Davies' narrative of the planting of the Popham Colony at the mouth of the Kennebec. This may account for the statement, made by Strachey for the first time, that the river discovered by Waymouth was the Sagadahoc.

"From hence we might discerne many Ilands, and the Maine Land, from the west-south-west to the east-north-east; and north-north-east from vs a great way as it then seemed (and as we after found it) vp into the Maine, we might discerne very high Mountaines, although the Maine seemed but lowe Land, which gave vs a hope," etc.[43]

Sir Ferdinando Gorges, in his Briefe Narration, published in London in 1658 (Maine Hist. Soc. Collections, Vol. 2, p. 17), says that Waymouth,

"Falling short of his course, happened into a river on the coast of America, called Pemaquid."[44]

Oldmixon, in his British Empire in America, published in London, in 1702, (Ed. of 1741, Vol. 1, p. 354,) says:

"The

---

43. The words "north-north-east from vs" are not found in Rosier's "Relation." It is a matter of no slight significance that twenty years after Waymouth's return to England, and before any discussion had arisen in reference to the harbor and river he discovered, just these words were here inserted, not as an editorial emendation, but as a part of the narrative. Evidently the reason for withholding the direction which existed in 1605 no longer existed, and the direction was accordingly now inserted in its proper place by authority.

44. Dr. Edward Ballard (Popham Memorial Volume, p. 313) says that Gorges here does not mean that the river was called Pemaquid, but the coast on which the "great river" was discovered; and he refers to Capt. John Smith's statement, already cited, which says that Waymouth's (Rosier's) "Relation" described "Pemmaquid." Manifestly, the reference here is to a tract of country called by that name. See the quotation on page 45.

WAYMOUTH'S VOYAGE, 1605.   51

"The trading Voyages of *Gosnold* and the Bristol men began to put the *English* on new Attempts for a Settlement; but before it could be brought to pass, Henry Earl of Southampton, and Thomas Lord Arundel of Wardour, fitted out a ship under the command of Capt. George Weymouth, who fell upon the Eastern Parts of Long Island (as 'tis now called) where they landed, and traffick'd with the Indians, made Trial of the Soil by *English* Grain; and found the Natives more affable and courteous than the Inhabitants of those other Parts of *Virginia* which the English had discover'd; but the Adventurers, being greedy of Gain, overreach'd the *Indians*, imposing on their Ignorance: of which they growing jealous, it occasion'd the many Murders and Massacres that follow in the Course of this History.

"Capt. *Weymouth* enter'd the River of Powhattan, southward of the Bay of Chesapeake. He sail'd up above forty miles, finding the channel deep and broad, being a Mile over, and 7 to 10 Fathom in Depth, having Creeks on every Side at every half mile Distance, all deep and safe, in which Ships of 500 Tons may ride in many Places, with a Cable on Shore in the soft Oaze."

Rev. William Hubbard, who died in 1704, in his General History of New England from the Discovery to 1660 (Cambridge Ed., 1815, p. 12), says Waymouth
"Discovered

"Discovered a great river in these parts supposed to be Kennebecke, neere unto Pemaquid."

"Beverly, in his History of Virginia, (2d Ed., London, 1722), refers in his preface to Oldmixon's British Empire, and its various errors requiring correction, etc., and says:

"Page 220, *He says that Captain* Weymouth *in* 1605, *enter'd* Powhatan *River* Southward *of the Bay* of Chesapeake; ——— *whereas* Powhatan *River is now call'd* James *River, and lies within the mouth of* Chesapeake *Bay some miles, on the West side of it; and Captain* Weymouth's *Voyage was only to* Hudson's *River*, which *is in* New York, *much Northward of the Capes of* Virginia."

But on page 11, with curious inconsistency, Beverly thus describes Waymouth's voyage:

"§ 12. In the Year 1605, a Voyage was made from *London* in a single Ship, with which they designed to fall in with the Land about the Latitude 39°; but the Winds put her a little further Northward, and she fell upon the Eastern Parts of *Long Island* (as it is now call'd, but all went then under the Name of *Virginia*). Here they traffick'd with the *Indians*, as the others had done before them; made short Trials of the Soil by *English* Grain, and found the *Indians*, as in other Places, very

very fair and courteous at first, till they got more Knowledge of the English, and perhaps thought themselves over-reached because one bought better Pennyworths than another; upon which afterwards they never fail'd to take Revenge as they found their Opportunity or Advantage. So this Company also return'd with the Ship, having ranged forty Miles up *Connecticut* River, and call'd the Harbour where they rid *Penticost* Harbour because of their Arrival there on Whitsunday."

Thomas Prince, in his Chronological History of New England (Boston, 1736, Part 1, p. 14,) referring to the river Waymouth entered, says in a note:

"This seems to be Sagadehock; and Sir F. Gorges doubtless mistakes in calling it Pemaquid River."

Rev. William Stith, who published his History of Virginia, in 1747, referring to Waymouth's voyage (Sabine's Reprint, pp. 33, 34,) says:

"What River this was, and what Parts of the American Coast they fell upon, is difficult to determine exactly. For their neglecting to tell us what Course they steered, after they were disengaged from the Shoals, renders it doubtful, whether they fell in with some part of Massachusetts Bay; or rather farther Southward, or the Coast of Rhode Island, Naraganset, or Connecticut; altho'

altho' I am most inclined to believe this river was either that of Naraganset or Connecticut, and the Island, what is now called Block Island."

Having made his guess, Stith proceeds to demolish that made by Oldmixon:

"According to his usual custom [Oldmixon] is here most egregiously bewildered and lost. For after having injudiciously enough determined the small Island they first made, of six miles in compass, to be Long Island on the Coast of New York, he immediately after, with still greater Obscurity and Grossness, calls this the River of Powhatan, now James River, to the Southward, as he says of the Bay of Chesapeake."

In 1797, Jeremy Belknap, D.D., who was about to prepare an article on Waymouth for his "American Biography," requested Capt. John Foster Williams, of the United States Revenue service, to examine the coast of Maine with reference to Waymouth's discoveries in 1605. Capt. Williams was furnished with an abstract of Rosier's "Relation," as found in Purchas His Pilgrimmes. In his reply (American Biography, Vol. 2, pp. 249–251), dated Boston, Oct. 1, 1797, Capt. Williams says:

"The first land Captain Weymouth saw, a whitish sandy

sandy cliff, W. N. W. six leagues, must have been Sankaty Head (Nantucket). With the wind at W. S. W. and S. S. W. he could have fetched into this bay (Boston), and must have seen Cape Cod had the weather been clear. But

"The land he saw on the 17th I think must be the island Monhegan, as no other island answers the description. In my last cruise to the east ward I sounded, and had thirty fathoms about one league to the northward of the island. The many islands he saw, and the mainland, extending from W. S. W. to the E. N. E., agree with that shore; the mountains he saw bearing N. N. E. were Penobscot *Hills* or *Mountains;* for, from the place where I suppose the ship lay at anchor, the above mountains bear N. N. E.

"The Harbour where he lay with his ship, and named Pentecost Harbour, is, I suppose, what is now called *George's Island Harbour*, which bears north from Monhegan about two leagues; which harbour and islands agree with his descriptions, I think, tolerably well, and the name, *George's Islands*, seems to confirm it.

"When the captain went in his boat and discovered a great river trending far up into the main, I suppose he went as far as Two Bush Island, about three or four leagues

leagues from the ship; from thence he could discover Penobscot Bay.

	Miles.
Distance from the ship to Two-Bush Island is about	10
From Two-Bush Island to Owl's Head,	9
From Owl's Head to the north end of Long Island,	27
From the north end of Long Island to Old Fort Pownal,	6
From the Old Fort to the head of the tide or falls in Penobscot River,	30
	82

"I suppose he went with his ship round Two-Bush Island, and then sailed up to the westward of Long Island, supposing himself to be then in the river, the mountains on the main to the westward extending near as high up as Belfast Bay. I think it probable that he anchored with his ship off the point which is now called the Old Fort Point.

"The codde of the river, where he went with his shallop, and marched up in the country towards the mountains, I think must be Belfast Bay.

"The canoe that came from the farther part of the codde of the river eastward, with Indians, I think it probable came from Bagaduce." Dr.

WAYMOUTH'S VOYAGE, 1605.   57

Dr. Belknap accepted Capt. Williams' view, and in his American Biography, published in 1794 (Harper's Ed., 1855, Vol. 2, p. 252), he writes:

"Weymouth's voyage is memorable only for the discovery of Penobscot River, and for the decoying of five of the natives on board his ship, whom he carried to England."

Abiel Holmes, in his American Annals (1805), Vol. 1, p. 130, refers to Waymouth's voyage, and in a note makes this citation:

"The discovery of which they seem to be proudest was that of a river, which they do on many accounts prefer to any known American river"; and Holmes adds: "Dr. Belknap, in his first volume of American Biography (See Harper's Ed., Vol. 1, p. 71,) says, this great river is supposed to be either Penobscot or Kennebeck; but before the publication of his second volume, he had satisfied himself, after careful examination and inquiry, that it was the Penobscot."

Capt. Williams' view, adopted by Belknap, was also adopted by Williamson in his History of the State of Maine, published in 1832. Waymouth, he says (Vol. 1, pp. 192, 193), named the harbor where he anchored after leaving Monhegan, "Pentecost Harbor, now George's Island

Island Harbor, a well known haven at the mouth of St. George's river." Leaving this harbor, "they proceeded northwardly, by estimation, sixty miles. In their progress up Penobscot Bay they came to anchor on the 12th not far from the land, abreast the high mountains, since called Penobscot hills [now Camden Heights]." The next day they reached "that part of the river which inclines more to the westward [probably Belfast bay, or possibly the waters between the lower part of Orphan Island and the main]."

In a discourse before the Maine Historical Society, at its annual meeting at Brunswick, Sept. 6, 1846, Hon. George Folsom, of New York, referred to Waymouth's voyage, and said, (Maine Hist. Soc. Collections, Vol. 2, p. 22), he "sailed up a noble river, now supposed to have been the Penobscot."

In 1857, John McKeen, Esq., of Brunswick, read before the Maine Historical Society a paper, in which he aimed to show that

"The Pentecost Harbour of Capt. Waymouth was what we now call Boothbay or Townsend, and not St. George's Island Harbour; and the river which he discovered and explored was the Sagadahock, and not the Penobscot." (See Maine Historical Soc. Collections, Vol. 5, p. 338.)

In

In his view, Waymouth ascended the Kennebec from its mouth, and at Merrymeeting Bay passed into the Androscoggin, "formerly the Pejepscot, and originally the continuation of the Sagadahock," p. 323.

Hon. William Willis, in the same volume of the Maine Historical Society's Collections, pp. 346–350, in an introduction to a letter from George Popham to King James I., declared his dissent from the views presented by Mr. McKeen, and advocated the earlier theory that the river Waymouth discovered was the Penobscot.

In 1859, R. K. Sewall, Esq., published his Ancient Dominions of Maine, in which he says, pp. 75, 76, that no one familiar with the localities can doubt "that the Pentecost Harbor of Weymouth is the Townsend or Boothbay Harbor." Waymouth, in his shallop, he holds, made his first excursion from Pentecost Harbor by "the inland passage northwesterly across or up the waters of the Sheepscot and the Bay of Hockomock, through to the Sagadahock, opposite Bath," where he discovered "a great river which he imagined ran 'far up into the land, by the breadth, depth and strong flood;' and following the broad reach of the mouth of the Androscoggin, which trends west into the main and flows from the White Mountains, he explored that river as a part of the Sagadahock."

Palfrey

Palfrey, in his History of New England, the first edition of which appeared in 1858, referring to Waymouth's Voyage (Vol. 1, p. 76, ed. of 1876), says: "Shifting his course to the north, he entered the Kennebec or the Penobscot River." In a note he adds: "The Kennebec agrees best with Waymouth's observation of the latitude."

For some time George Prince, of Bath, had been in doubt whether either the Kennebec or the Penobscot theory was tenable, and Mr. McKeen's paper led him to investigate the subject anew. He says (pamphlet on Rosier's Narrative, Bath, 1860, p. 1):

"In the summer of 1858, while reading Rosier's Narrative of Waymouth's voyage in 1605 to the coast of Maine, as published in the eighth volume of the Mass. Hist. Col., kindly loaned me by the librarian of the Maine Hist. Society, the suspicions which I had before entertained were confirmed, viz., that the forty mile river there referred to, instead of being as all writers and historians had heretofore supposed, either the Kennebec or Penobscot, was none other than the George's, the mouth of which is about 50 miles from that of the Penobscot, and some 30 miles from the Kennebec. Accordingly in August, 1858, I published an article in a weekly paper published in Thomaston, taking the above ground, and giving my reasons therefor."

The

WAYMOUTH'S VOYAGE, 1605.

The favorable reception which the new theory received, together with the urgent request of members of the Maine Historical Society, led Mr. Prince to prepare a paper, which was read before the Society at a meeting held in Augusta, in January, 1859, and which afterwards was published in the sixth volume of the Society's Collections. He also published, in 1860, the pamphlet from which the above citation is taken, in which he presented his views in connection with Rosier's "Relation," reprinted from Vol. VIII., 3d Series, Mass. Hist. Society's Collections, and illustrated by a map of St. George's Harbor and River.

At a meeting of the Maine Historical Society in June of the same year, Rev. David Cushman, of Warren, read a paper, in which he took the same position as Mr. Prince. A part of this paper also appears in Maine Hist. Society's Collections, Vol. VI., pp. 293–318.

But the long controversy was not settled. Rev. Edward Ballard, of Brunswick, prepared a paper for the Memorial Volume, containing the proceedings at the Popham Celebration, August 29, 1862, in which, pp. 301–317, he aimed to identify the river which Waymouth discovered with the Kennebec, and Pentecost Harbor with Boothbay Harbor.

Eaton, in his History of Thomaston, published in 1865,

1865, refers to Waymouth's voyage, and says (Vol. 1, p. 14):

"Two days after [his arrival at Monhegan], begin Whitsunday, Weymouth sailed two or three leagues farther north among the 'islands more adjoining to the main, and *in the road directly with the mountains*,' and entered 'a goodly haven,' which he named Pentecost Harbor, now known as St. George's Island Harbor."

The river which Waymouth discovered, in his opinion, was the St. George's River.

In his History of Bristol, Bremen and Pemaquid, published in 1873, Prof. Johnston (pp. 29-34) discusses quite fully the points in dispute concerning Pentecost Harbor and the river discovered by Waymouth. Having presented the various theories, he says (p. 33):

"The suggestion of Mr. Prince, that the George's river is the 'true river of Weymouth' though still rejected by some, will probably, eventually, be accepted as a satisfactory settlement of this long debated question. Rosier's description of Weymouth's river applies well to this; very much better certainly, than to any other on the coast of New England."

Samuel A. Drake, in his Nooks and Corners of the New England Coast, published in 1875, has a chapter on

WAYMOUTH'S VOYAGE, 1605.   63

on "Monhegan Island." Referring to Waymouth's anchorage north of Monhegan, he says (p. 105):

"The main-land possessed greater attraction for Weymouth. Thinking his anchorage insecure, he brought his vessel the next day to the islands 'more adjoining to the main,' and in the road directly with the mountains, about three leagues from the island where he had first anchored.

"I read this description while standing on the deck of the *Katahdin*, and found it to answer admirably the conditions under which I then surveyed the land. We were near enough to make out the varied features of a long line of sea-coast stretching northward for many a mile. There were St. George's Islands, three leagues distant, and more adjoining to the main. And there were the Camden Mountains in the distance."[45]

Ex-Gov. J. L. Chamberlain, in his address delivered at the Centennial Exposition, in Philadelphia, Nov. 4, 1876, referring to Waymouth's voyage, says (p. 24):

"In his superb ship the 'Archangel' he came to anchor under Monhegan, whence he visited the mainland and

---

45. In a note he says: "A good many arguments may be found in the 'Collections of the Maine Historical Society,' as to whether Weymouth ascended the Penobscot or the Kennebec. All assume Monhegan to have been the first island seen. This being conceded, the landmarks given in the text follow, without reasonable ground for controversy."

and explored what Strachey calls 'the excellent and beneficial river of Sagadahoc,' and afterwards it would seem the regions of the Penobscot."

Hon. Jos. Williamson, in his History of Belfast, (1877) rejects the Kennebec theory. He says (p. 31, 32):

"To any one familiar with the coast of Maine, it is evident that this position cannot be sustained. The absence of the 'very high mountains,' referred to by Rosier, in the vicinity of that river, is alone sufficient to negative it. Mr. McKeen contends that they were the White Mountains, which are occasionally seen from Monhegan. Yet, after going up the river and landing, Waymouth's party judged these mountains to be 'within a league of them.' They are over twenty times that distance removed.

"Many of the indications noticed by Rosier are irreconcilable with the Penobscot theory, and suggest that Dr. Belknap and Capt. Williams found their conclusions on a misapprehension of the facts and localities. So experienced a navigator as Capt. Waymouth could hardly have mistaken Penobscot Bay, which is over ten miles wide at Belfast Bay, for a river which beareth in breadth a mile, some times three-quarters and half a mile the narrowest. . . . . The mountains, which were kept constantly in sight, from the time of reaching Monhegan,

gan, would have been left far astern, yet, after landing in the 'codde of the river,' they marched directly towards them. There is wanting to Penob. Bay and River the 'very gallant coves on both sides, every half mile.' . . . The fact that the river does not trend 'westward into the main,' but in an opposite direction, seems alone to destroy the Penob. theory.

"Perhaps the more satisfactory solution of this much mooted question is that given by Capt. George Prince, of Bath, who, in 1858, published the reasons for his conviction that the George's River was the scene of Waymouth's explorations."

June 5, 1878, the Rev. B. F. DeCosta, D. D., of New York, read a paper before the New England Historic-Genealogical Society in Boston, on "The Expeditions of Weymouth and Popham, 1605-8." Waymouth, he said,

"Upon his first exploration, visited the Kennebec, going up the Sheepscot passage, as did Champlain in 1605, and Biencourt in 1611, emerging through opposite Bath, returning down the main stream, and ascending from its mouth to Boothbay. Afterward he went down to the mouth again with his ship, and ascended in the regular way to the neighborhood of Bath, computing the distance at twenty-six miles. The account of of the voyage referred to the 'codde' of the river beyond the ship. This was Merrymeeting Bay, at the eastern end of which he landed, and marched toward the hills seen continually at their arrival on the coast, and which, when at the bay, they judged to be close at hand. The boat journey was extended up the Kennebec, and upon returning in the ship, as was related in the narrative, seven hours were required to reach the mouth of the river. By those treating the subject in a simple method, a perfectly harmonious result was obtained, giving these slightly obscure phrases their proper meaning, and changing the word 'westward,' which had been taken to refer to the Androscoggin, and was undoubtedly a clerical error to 'northward,' and by throwing out the White Mountains west of the Kennebec, the arguments in favor of the Kennebec theory were disembarrassed and had their full weight."[46]

As many of the members of the Maine Historical Society were not familiar with the localities mentioned in the discussion of Waymouth's discovery, the Field-Day excursion, August 20–22, 1879, was so arranged as to give them an opportunity of visiting Monhegan and Boothbay,

---

46. This is a quotation from a report of the paper in the *Boston Daily Advertiser* of June 6, 1878. Dr. De Costa, to whom I applied, was unable to furnish me with a copy of his paper, but certified to the correctness of the report as far as it went.

Boothbay, and of exploring the passage to Bath by way of the Sheepscot and the Sasanoa River. At a meeting of the Society in May, 1881, R. K. Sewall, Esq., of Wiscasset, read a report of this excursion, in which he reaffirmed the views he had already expressed in his "Ancient Dominions of Maine." Some of the members of the Society, however, who participated in the Field-Day excursion of 1879 were unable to make the Kennebec theory harmonize with Rosier's narrative; and the wish was expressed by those who were familiar with St. George's Harbor and St. George's River that the Society should visit these waters for further investigations. Such a visit was included in the Field-Day excursion of September, 1881. The use of the Revenue Cutter Dallas was secured through the courtesy of the Secretary of the Treasury, and both the St. George's River and St. George's Harbor were visited. A report of this excursion was presented by the writer at the meeting of the Society early in 1882, with the reasons that led him to adopt the view that St. George's Harbor is the Pentecost Harbor of Rosier's "Relation," and that the river which Waymouth discovered was the St. George's River.

In the earlier editions of his History of the United States, Bancroft, following Williamson and others, says Waymouth "ascended the west branch of the Penobscot

scot beyond Belfast Bay." But two letters to Hon. Wm. Willis, of Portland, among the Willis manuscripts (63 and 64 in Vol. A,) in the Public Library, Portland, dated Oct. 21 and 22, 1857, show that at that time he was re-studying the subject. In the new (1883) edition of his History (Vol. 1, pp. 81, 82,) he says, concerning Waymouth's discovery:

"Weighing anchor on Easter Sunday, 1605, on the fourteenth of May he came near the whitish, sandy promontory of Cape Cod. To escape the continual shoals in which he found himself embayed, he stood out to sea, then turned to the north, and on the seventeenth anchored to the north of Monhegan Island, in sight of hills to the nort-north-east on the main. On Whit-Sunday he found his way among the St. George's Islands into an excellent harbor which was accessible by four passages, defended from all winds, and had good mooring upon a clay ooze, and even upon the rocks by the cliff side. . . . Having in the last of May discovered in his pinnace the broad, deep current of the St. George's, on the eleventh of June, Waymouth, with a gentle wind, passed up with the ship into the river for about eighteen miles, which were reckoned six and twenty, and 'all consented in joy' to admire its width of a half mile or a mile," etc.

In

In the Magazine of American History (Vol. 9, p. 300,) in a notice of Mr. Bancroft's revised first volume, the Rev. B. F. De Costa, D. D., of New York, says Bancroft makes Waymouth anchor "'in an excellent harbor,' among the St. George's Islands, on the coast of Maine, where there is no harbor, as all but blind men visiting the coast may see. He afterwards sends Waymouth to explore a splendid river in a region where there is so little water that fish can hardly swim."

To this criticism, Mr. Bancroft replied (Magazine of Am. History, Vol. 9, pp. 459, 460):

"As to the voyage of Waymouth in 1605, the account of its landfall and discoveries was revised after the most careful inquiry. John McKeen, of Brunswick, Maine, proved beyond a doubt that the old theory, that Waymouth entered the Penobscot, could not be maintained. George Prince, of Bath, confirmed by David Cushman, of Warren, decided that the island which he struck was Monhegan, that the group of islands among which he passed was the St. George's; that the river which he entered was the St. George's. I have private letters from Maine to the same effect; but, to leave no room for uncertainty, I went to my friend Mr. Bache, then the chief of the Coast Survey, and he and the surveyors specially employed by him in the survey of that part

part of the coast of Maine, explained to me that beyond a doubt Waymouth touched at Monhegan Island, that the mountains which he writes that he saw at the east-north-east were the Camden mountains, that the islands through which he passed were the St. George's Islands, that the river which he ascended was the river of St. George.

"The Magazine of April sets forth that I send Waymouth where there is no harbor. I have been again to the Coast Survey, and asked if there are harbors in that region, and the answer was 'good harbors in abundance.' As to the depth of the river, which the Magazine represents as having so little water that fish can barely swim in it, the Coast Survey chart tells the very different story that there is a river of great uniform depth. Any one who knows the coast of Maine, and reads the decription of Waymouth [Rosier] with the charts of the Coast Survey before him, will see that the case is clear beyond a question."

In a reply to Mr. Bancroft (Magazine of Am. History, Vol. 10, pp. 143–145), Dr. De Costa said:

"A true interpretation of Waymouth's [Rosier's] narrative will carry the investigation to the Kennebec; while there is independent testimony which settles the question

question beyond doubt. This testimony was not adduced until long after Mr. Bancroft published his early volumes. Originally it was supposed that the Penobscot was the river discovered. Belknap furnished a captain in the revenue service with portions of Waymouth's narrative, which he took with him to the main coast, and after examination, reported that Waymouth visited the Penobscot. In time the error was detected, and the next river adopted was the St. George's, which, in turn, was abandoned by the majority of investigators. Ultimately, however, the history of Strachey was printed from the manuscript preserved in the British Museum, and now we have the direct testimony of Waymouth's cotemporary, who knew all the facts of the case, and distinctly declares that Waymouth discovered the Kennebec, then known as the 'benyficial river of Sagadahoc.' Finally, a passage in the neglected works of Champlain was pointed out confirming the statement of Strachey, Champlain having entered the Kennebec only nine days after Waymouth left the river, and there the Frenchman heard of the five savages of the Kennebec who were captured by the English explorer. The St. George's theory was framed and adopted before this conclusive testimony of Strachey and Champlain had come to light; and if these facts had been known at the

outset

outset there would never have been any wrong interpretation of the narrative."[47]

Rev. Henry O. Thayer, in a paper on the Popham Colony, read before the Maine Historical Society Dec. 22, 1885, establishes "at the George's Islands the Pentecost Harbor of the vexing voyage of Waymouth;" and adds, "This location of Pentecost Harbor cannot be successfully

---

[47]. In this statement, to which Mr. Bancroft made no reply, Dr. De Costa has fallen into several errors which this review of the literature of Waymouth's voyage enables me to correct. When it was discovered that the Penobscot theory was untenable, the St. George's was not "the next river adopted," as Dr. De Costa says, but the Kennebec, as the citations already presented show. It is difficult to imagine on what ground Dr. De Costa states that the St. George's theory "was abandoned by the majority of investigators." On the contrary, it seems to have found increasing favor, and the testimony of the Portland *Advertiser* of Aug. 6, 1883, quoted in the Magazine of American History, Vol. 10, p. 202, is worthy of notice, as it refers to Dr. De Costa's reply to Mr. Bancroft. Referring to the view of Mr. Bancroft that the St. George's theory best fulfills the conditions of the narrative of the voyage, the *Advertiser* says this "is the conclusion of most of the members of the Maine Historical Society after visiting the ground, book in hand, and comparing the two theories."

As to Dr. De Costa's statement that "the St. George's theory was framed and adopted before the conclusive testimony of Strachey and Champlain had come to light," an examination of the facts shows that so far as Strachey is concerned this is an error. Strachey's narrative appeared in the third volume of the Maine Historical Society's Collections, which was printed in 1853. Prince read his paper before the Maine Historical Society in 1858, and in his pamphlet published in 1860 he refers to Strachey as "the first to mislead in this matter," and devotes a page to his statements. If the narrative of Champlain's Voyages had been in Prince's hands it would have enabled him to strengthen his position.

successfully assailed when there is fair dealing with Rosier's narrative."

SUMMARY.

What facts does this survey of the literature of Waymouth's voyage suggest? I submit the following:

1. In the three earliest records in which a reference to Waymouth's voyage is found, there are no indications that Waymouth in his ship was west of Pemaquid. In the narrative of Champlain's voyages it is said that when Champlain was in the Kennebec, Waymouth was at an island which, from the description, is recognized as Monhegan by all writers on the subject, so far as I am aware. In the narrative of the Popham Colony, found by Dr. De Costa in the library of Lambeth Palace, London, it is stated that a cross, set up by Waymouth as was supposed, was found on an island which the colonists called St. George's Island. De Costa and others think the island was Monhegan, but statements in the narrative, as already indicated, make this impossible, and point rather to one of the St. George's Islands, probably Allen's Island. Capt. John Smith, who was on the coast of Maine in 1614, and was well acquainted with

with the Kennebec, refers to Waymouth without connecting him with that river, but simply states that Waymouth was at Pemaquid, which he says in another place was opposite Monhegan.

2. Strachey, who never was on the coast of Maine, but prepared his "Historie" with the Relations of Rosier and Davies before him, was the first—writing, it is believed, in 1618—to suggest that the river discovered by Waymouth was the Kennebec.

3. Purchas, who published his "Pilgrimmes," in 1625, in reproducing Rosier's Relation, amends the narrative by inserting the direction of the high mountains toward which Waymouth went in passing up the river he discovered. There was then no longer any reason, as there was after Waymouth's return to England, why the direction should be withheld, and its insertion by Purchas must have been with authority. Following the direction indicated, Waymouth could have entered neither the Kennebec nor the Penobscot, but must have sailed up the George's River.

4. Gorges, writing late in life, and who therefore had long been familiar with matters pertaining to the discovery and colonization of the country, mentions Waymouth as happening "into a river on the coast of America, called Pemaquid."

5. Hubbard

5. Hubbard, who was the next to refer to Waymouth's voyage—he died in 1704—says Waymouth discovered a great river "supposed to be Kennebecke neere unto Pemaquid."

6. Oldmixon, in a work published at the beginning of the eighteenth century, and with a singular disregard of the requirements of the "Relation," claimed that Waymouth entered the Powhatan, now known as the James River. Beverly, criticizing Oldmixon not long after, affirmed in one part of his history that Waymouth entered the Hudson River, and with a curious inconsistency in another part, said that he entered the Connecticut River; while Stith, about the middle of the eighteenth century, adding his guess, thought it might be the Connecticut or the Narragansett.

7. Prince, in his Chronological History of New England, Boston, 1736, followed Strachey and Hubbard, yet not with entire confidence. The river Waymouth entered, he said, "seems to be Sagadehock, and Sir F. Gorges doubtless mistakes in calling it Pemaquid River."

8. This lack of confidence Belknap shared in a larger degree, and recognizing the importance of a careful investigation, he secured in 1797 the aid of Capt. Williams, of the U. S. Revenue Service, who proceeded in his vessel to the coast of Maine, where from a study of

Rosier's

Rosier's "Relation," as found in "Purchas His Pilgrimmes," he came to the conclusion that St. George's Harbor was Pentecost Harbor, and the Penobscot the river Waymouth discovered. This view was subsequently adopted by Williamson and later writers down to the middle of this century.

9. In 1857, John McKeen, in a paper read before the Maine Historical Society, rejecting the Penobscot theory as untenable, advocated the view that the Pentecost Harbor of Rosier's narrative was Boothbay Harbor, and that the river which Waymouth ascended was the Kennebec, from which he passed into the Androscoggin.

10. George Prince, in a paper read before the Maine Historical Society in 1859, presented objections to the view advocated by Mr. McKeen, and insisted that Pentecost Harbor was the present St. George's Harbor, and that the river which Waymouth discovered was the St. George's River.

11. This view was accepted by Rev. David Cushman and others; also by officers of the United States Coast Survey, who at the request of Mr. Bancroft gave special attention to the subject, and was adopted by Mr. Bancroft in the subsequent edition of his History of the United States.

12. The Kennebec theory has retained a few earnest advocates

advocates to the present time; but nothing is more evident than that the St. George's theory is regarded by a constantly increasing number as meeting far more satisfactorily the requirements of the " Relation."

A
TRVE RELATION

of the most prosperous voyage

made this present yeere 1605,
by Captaine George Waymouth,
in the Discouery of the land
of Virginia:

Where he discouered 60 miles vp
a most excellent Riuer; together with a most
fertile land.

Written by James Rosier,
a Gentleman employed
in the voyage.

LONDONI
Impensis Geor. Bishop.
1605.

THOMAS ARUNDEL,

BARON OF WARDOUR,

OBIT 1639.

TO THE READER.

BEING employed in this Voyage by the right honourable Thomas Arundell[48] Baron of Warder, to take due notice, and make true report of the discouery therein performed: I became very diligent to obserue (as much as I could) whatsoeuer was materiall or of consequence in the businesse which I collected into this briefe summe, intending upon our returne to publish the same. But he soone changed the course of his intendments; and long before our arriuall in England had so farre engaged himselfe with the Archduke,[49] that he was constrained to relinquish this action.

---

48. Thomas Arundell was elevated to the peerage May 4, 1605, on the occasion of the christening of Mary, third daughter of James I., the first princess of the new dynasty born in England. In honor of that event, many peers were raised to higher rank, and numbers of knights were created barons.

49. The reference is to the Archduke Albert, a son of Maximilian II. and a brother of the Emperor Rudolph

action. But the commodities and profits of the countrey, together with the fitnesse of plantation, being by some honourable Gentlemen of good woorth and qualitie, and Merchants[50] of good sufficiency and judgment duly considered, haue at their owne charge (intending both their priuate and the common benefit of their countrey) vndertaken the transporting of a Colony for the plantation thereof ;[51] being much encouraged thereunto by the gracious

II. He had been Archbishop of Toledo, but had resigned his spiritual office, and was now ruling the Netherlands, of which he was made Governor in 1596. He married the Infanta Isabella Anne in 1599. Under date of 1605, in his History of the United Netherlands, (Vol. 4, p. 228) Motley says, "Considerable levies of troops were made in England by the Archduke." In August, 1605, Arundell was appointed Colonel of one of the English Regiments thus raised, and in disguise crossed over to Holland against the will of King James, who was highly displeased and ordered him to be recalled. Winwood's State papers ii, 59, iii, 144. As Governor of the Netherlands Albert was so well known in England that it was not necessary for Rosier to designate him otherwise than as "the Archduke."

50. The credit of this expedition has been given by some writers to the Muscovia and Turkey Companies. This is an error. Waymouth himself, strangely enough, was the first to put this error on record. It has recently been shown that the East India Fellowship offered to share the enterprise with the Muscovia Company on equal terms. The latter, however, claimed the sole right and privilege of navigating the northern seas and declined the offer. The East India Fellowship appealed to the Privy Council, and later the Muscovia Company receded from its position and offered to unite with the East India Fellowship in fitting out the expedition; but the offer was not accepted. See Hakluyt Society's "Voyages toward the North-west," pp. 51-55.

51. Prominent among them were Sir Ferdinando Gorges and Sir John Popham, Lord Chief Justice of England. Sir Ferdinando, in August of the following year, fitted out a vessel, under the command of Henry Chal.

gracious fauour of the KINGS MAIESTY himselfe, and diuers Lords of his Highnesse most Honourable Priuie Councell. After these purposed designes were concluded, I was animated to publish this briefe Relation, and not before; because some forrein Nation (being fully assured of the fruitfulnesse of the countrie) haue hoped

long, to whom were assigned two of the natives brought over by Waymouth. Challong was instructed to keep a northerly course to Cape Breton, and then to follow the coast southward "till they found by the natives they were near the place they were assigned to." But the Captain was taken sick not long after leaving port, and the ship's course was then shaped for the West Indies. There, says Gorges, the vessel was captured by a Spanish fleet from Havana, "and carried into Spain, where their ship and goods were confiscated, themselves made prisoners, the voyage overthrown, and both of my natives lost." Not long after Challong's departure, Sir John Popham sent out another vessel, of which Thomas Hanham was commander and Martin Pring, of Bristol, who had been on the coast of Massachusetts, in 1603, was master. They were to second Challong in the proposed discovery. At least one of the Indians brought to England by Waymouth accompanied the expedition. Gorges' instructions were followed, and the vessel arrived safely at the designated locality. Not finding Challong, they made "a perfect discovery of all those rivers and harbors" to which their attention had been directed by Gorges, and then returned to England. Their's, says Gorges (Maine Hist. Society's Collections, Vol. 2, p. 19), was "the most exact discovery of that coast that ever came to my hands"; and the report brought back by them made such an impression on Sir John Popham, Gorges and their associates, that the Popham Colony was sent out in the following year. The Plymouth Company, in a relation published subsequently, say of this report: "Upon whose relations afterwards, the lord chief justice and we all waxed so confident of the business, that the year following every man of any worth, formerly interested in it, was willing to join in the charge for the sending over a competent number of people to lay the ground of a hopeful plantation.'

hoped hereby to gaine some knowledge of the place, seeing they could not allure our Captaine or any speciall man of our Company to combine with them for their direction, nor obtaine their purpose, in conueying away our Saluages, which was busily in practise. And this is the cause that I haue neither written of the latitude or variation most exactly obserued by our Captaine with sundrie instruments, which together with his perfect Geographicall Map of the countrey, he entendeth hereafter to set forth. I haue likewise purposedly omitted here to adde a collection of many words in their language to the number of foure or fiue hundred, as also the names of diuers of their gouernours, as well their friends as their enemies: being reserued to be made knowen for the benefit of those that shal goe in the next Voyage. But our particular proceedings in the whole Discouerie, the commodious situation of the Riuer, the fertilitie of the land, with the profits there to be had, and here reported, I refer to be uerified by the whole Company, as being eye-witnesses of my words, and most of them neere inhabitants upon the Thames. So with my prayers to God for the conuersion of so ingenious and well-disposed people, and for the prosperous successive euents of the noble intenders the prosecution thereof, I rest

      Your friend   I. R.

A TRUE RELATION

of Captaine George Waymouth his Voyage, made this present yeere 1605; in the Discouerie of the North part of Virginia.

PON Tuesday the 5 day of March, about ten a clocke afore noone, we set saile from Ratcliffe,[52] and came to an anker that tide about two a clocke before Grauesend.[53]

From thence the 10 of March being Sunday at night we

---

52. Ratcliffe was a hamlet on the Thames, east of London, in the parish of Stepney, and was inhabited principally by sea-faring men. Ratcliffe Highway, which connected the village with the metropolis, was the Regent Street of London sailors, who, according to an old authority, never extended their walks beyond this semi-marine region. It is said by some to have derived its name from the red cliff, or bank of the river Thames, at this point. Others, more correctly perhaps, connect the name with the manor of Ratcliffe in the parish of Stepney.

53. Gravesend is thirty miles below London on the Thames. It occurs in Doomsday Book as Gravesham. It was burned by the French in 1377. In 1573 it obtained a charter of incorporation from Queen Elizabeth.

we ankered in the Dounes:[54] and there rode til the next day about three a clocke after noone, when with a scant winde we set saile; and by reason the winde continued Southwardly, we were beaten vp and doune: but on Saturday the 16 day about foure a clocke after noon we put into Dartmouth Hauen,[55] where the continuance of the winde at South & Southwest constrained vs to ride till the last of this moneth. There we shipped some of our men and supplied necessaries for our Ship and Voyage.

Vpon Easter day we put to sea.

Upon Easter day, being the last of March, the winde comming at North, North East, about fiue a clocke after noone we wayed anker, and put to sea, In the name of God, being well victualled and furnished with munition and all necessaries: Our whole Company being but 29 persons; of whom I may boldly say few voyages have been manned forth with better Sea-men generally in respect of our small number.

Our Comnie 29 persons.

Munday the next day, being the first of Aprill, by sixe

---

54. A body of water north of Dover between Goodwin Sands and the main land.

55. Dartmouth is an ancient seaport of England, 31 miles S. of Exeter, and 229 miles S. W. of London. It is a small town, but once occupied an important place in the history of England. It was the rendezvous of the Crusaders' fleet in 1190, and in 1346–47 contributed 31 ships in the siege of Calais under Edward III. Several expeditions to the new world sailed from its harbor.

NORTH PART OF VIRGINIA. 87

sixe a clocke in the morning we were sixe leagues South-South-East from the Lizarde.[56]

At two a clocke in the afternoone this day, the weather being very faire, our Captaine for his owne experience and others with him sounded, and had five and fiftie fathoms and a halfe. The sounding was some small blacke perrie sand,[57] some reddish sand, a match or two, with small shels called Saint James his Shels.[58] The

Sounding.

56. The most southern promontory of England, 24 miles S. E. of the Land's End. Here are now two lofty light-houses.

57. This should doubtless read " blacke *ferric* sand." This is sand mingled with grains of magnetic iron ore, which make it black. Such sand is found in many localities, as *e. g.*, on one of the islands in Moosehead Lake.

58. For the following note, I am indebted to the late Prof. Charles E. Hamlin, of Cambridge, Mass.: " In the Middle Ages, pilgrims to the Holy Sepulchre at Jerusalem, returning, wore upon their hats or breasts, as proof that the pilgrimage had been accomplished, the shell of a cockle (*Cardium*), or of one of two kinds of scallop (*Pecten*),—indigenous to the Mediterranean. These were undoubtedly chosen as being both conspicuous and ornamental. The favorite was one of the scallops, of which more anon. The association of the name of St. James with the scallop owes its origin to a Spanish legend, of which the following is the substance: St. James, Patron of all Spain, if Catholic accounts may be trusted, has rested for nine hundred years in the Metropolitan church of Compostella (in full, Santiago de Compostella, *i. e.* Saint Jago or Saint James of Compostella), formerly capital of the province of Galicia. The legend has it that when the body of the saint was being miraculously conveyed in a ship without sails or oars, from Joppa to Galicia, it passed the village of Bonzas, on the coast of Portugal, on the day that a marriage had been celebrated there. The bridegroom and his friends were amusing themselves on horseback upon the sands, when his horse became unmanageable and plunged into the sea; whereupon the miraculous ship stopped in its voyage, and pres-

The foureteenth of Aprill being Sunday, betweene nine and ten of the clocke in the morning our Captaine descried

ently the bridegroom emerged, horse and man, close beside it. A conversation ensued between the knight and the saint's disciples on board, in which they apprized him that it was the saint who saved him from a watery grave, and explained to him the Christian religion. He believed and was baptized then and there, and immediately the ship resumed its voyage; while the knight came galloping back over the sea to rejoin his astonished friends. He told them all that had happened, and they, too, were converted, and the knight baptized his bride with his own hand. Now when the knight emerged from the sea, both his dress and the trappings of his horse were covered with scallop shells; and, therefore, the Galicians took the scallop shell as the sign of St. James. The favorite pilgrim badge was one of two kinds of Mediterranean *Pecten*. That which Linnæus connected with the legend of St. James, by giving to it the specific name *Jacobœus* (*Pecten Jacobœus*), is not found in the English Channel, where the St. James' shells were found by Waymouth. The other species, *Pecten opercularis*, smaller and less striking than the former, but yet beautiful, occurs in the Mediterranean, on the Atlantic coast of Spain and Portugal and in the English Channel. So that while Linnæus, in the name *Jacobœus*, points to the scallop oftenest chosen for the badge of pilgrimage, as being the original St. James' shell, the Spanish legend probably refers to *Pecten opercularis*. This is, however, immaterial, for no doubt the saint's name was in time bestowed upon all European species of scallop. Perfect specimens of any *Pecten* are beautiful objects, and have always been popular favorites. Some Roman and Pompeian sculptures bear the scallop shell, as do stone and leaden coffins of the Roman period, which have been dug up in England. And curiously enough, one writer states that Japanese pilgrims to the often pictured cone of Fusiyama wear upon the sleeve scallop shells as their badge. Our own New England *Pecten irradians*, Lamarck (the *Pecten concentricus* of Say), found abundantly at New Bedford and in Narragansett Bay, is much used in making pin-cushions and other ornamental work. A pretty species from the East Indies is often mounted for scarf-pins."

NORTH PART OF VIRGINIA. 89

descried the Iland Cuerno :⁵⁹ which bare South-West and by West, about seuen leagues from vs: by eleuen of the clocke we descried Flores⁶⁰ to the Southward of Cuerno, as it lieth: by foure a clocke in the afternoone we brought Cuerno, due South from vs within two leagues of the shore, but we touched not, because the winde was faire, and we thought our selues sufficiently watered and wooded. *We fell with the Ilands of Azores.*

Heere our Captaine obserued the Sunne, and found himselfe in the latitude of 40 degrees and 7 minutes: so he judged the North part of Cuerno to be in 40 degrees. After we had kept our course about a hundred leagues from the Ilands, by continuall Southerly windes we were forced and driuen from the Southward, whither we first intended. And when our Captaine by long beating saw it was but in vaine to striue with windes, not knowing Gods purposes heerein to our further blessing, (which after by his especiall direction wee found) he thought best to stand as nigh as he could by the winde to recouer what land we might first discouer.

Munday, the 6 of May, being in the latitude of 39 and a halfe about ten a clocke afore noone, we came to a riplin,

59. A small island, now Corvo, belonging to the Azores. Its present population is 1,000.

60. Another of the Azores group. It derives its name from the abundance of flowers that find shelter in its deep ravines. The present population is 10,508.

a riplin,[61] which we discerned a head our ship, which is a breach of water caused either by a fall, or by some meeting of currents, which we judged this to be; for the weather being very faire, and a small gale of winde, we sounded and found no ground in a hundred fathoms.

Munday, the 13 of May, about eleuen a clocke afore noone, our Captaine, judging we were not farre from land, sounded, and had a soft oaze in a hundred and sixty fathomes. At fowre a clocke after noone we sounded againe, and had the same oaze in a hundred fathoms.

From ten a clocke that night till three a clocke in the morning, our Captaine tooke in all sailes and lay at hull, being desirous to fall with the land in the day time, because it was an unknowen coast, which it pleased God in his

---

61. In 1877, the Superintendent of the U. S. Coast Survey directed Master Platt, U. S. N., to make a series of close observations on the direction and velocity of the currents between Nantucket Shoals and Cape Sable. In his report Master Platt refers to strong and well-marked tide-rips, which were noticed during the strength of the flood and ebb, and are described as looking like breakers in shoal water. He says: "When Latitude 42° N., Longitude 66° 30′ W., we saw what looked like shoal water or breakers ahead, but on sounding found one hundred and seventeen fathoms. We drifted along with the current until we came among these apparent breakers, and found them to be caused by a very heavy tide-rip. The sea was so high and 'cramming,' that we were obliged to reduce sail, three-reef the mainsail, and haul the boom well out to save our mainmast. These heavy tide-rips are nearly always well marked, and a stranger coming among them, especially at night, would be apt to be very much alarmed." Atlantic Local Coast Pilot, Sub-Division 3, Appendix, p. 11.

NORTH PART OF VIRGINIA.

in his mercy to grant vs, otherwise we had run our ship vpon the hidden rockes and perished all. For when we set saile we sounded in 100 fathoms: and by eight a clock, hauing not made aboue fiue or six leagues, our Captaine vpon a sudden change of water (supposing verily he saw the sand) presently sounded, and had but fiue fathoms. Much maruelling because we saw no land, he sent one to the top, who thence descried a whitish sandy cliffe,[62] which bare West-North-West about six leagues off from vs: but comming neerer within three or fowre leagues, we saw many breaches still neerer the land: at last we espied a great breach a head vs al along the shore, into which before we should enter,

62. Sighting Sankaty Head, a steep sandy cliff on the eastern extremity of Nantucket, and the most remarkable feature of the eastern shore of the island, Waymouth approached the Great Rip, and ran on to Rose and Crown Shoal. Two fathom spots near the southern part of the Rose and Crown are found upon the Coast Survey chart, eleven nautical miles E. by S. ½ S. from Sankaty Head Light, in Latitude 41° 15½'. *Vide* a communication by Henry Mitchel in the *Nantucket Enquirer* of June 22, 1882. Capt. John F. Williams, who, in 1797, at the request of Jeremy Belknap, made a study of Rosier's Relation, says

(American Biography, Hubbard's Ed., Vol. 2, p. 249), "The first land Capt Waymouth saw, a whitish sandy cliff W. N. W. six leagues, must have been Sankaty Head." In the Coast Survey Pilot from Boston to New York, p. 82, occurs the following: "Nantucket Island is surrounded by shoals, those especially which lie to the eastward of it making it one of the most dreaded parts of the coast. These shifting sandy shores, which extend in a south-easterly direction from the south-eastern end of the island, have various depths upon them, ranging from six feet to four fathoms, and change their positions more or less after every heavy gale."

enter, our Captaine thought best to hoist out his ship boate and sound it. Which if he had not done, we had beene in great danger: for he bare vp the ship, as neere as he durst after the boate: vntill Thomas Cam, his mate, being in the boat, called to him to tacke about & stand off, for in this breach he had very showld water, two fathoms and lesse vpon rockes, and sometime they supposed they saw the rocke within three or fowre foote, whereon the sea made a very strong breach: which we might discerne (from the top) to run along as we sailed by it 6 or 7 leagues to the Southward. This was in the latitude of 41 degrees, 20 minuts: wherefore we were constrained to put backe againe from the land: and sounding, (the weather being very faire and a small winde) we found our selues embaied with continuall showldes and rockes in a most uncertaine ground, from fiue or sixe fathoms, at the next cast of the lead we should haue 15 & 18 fathoms. Ouer many which we passed, and God so blessed vs, that we had wind and weather as faire as poore men in this distresse could wish: whereby we both perfectly discerned euery breach, and with the winde were able to turne, where we saw most hope of safest passage. Thus we parted from the land, which we had not so much before desired, and at the first sight rejoiced, as now we all joifully
praised

NORTH PART OF VIRGINIA.

praised God, that it had pleased him to deliuer vs from so imminent danger.

Heere we found great store of excellent Cod fish, and saw many Whales, as we had done two or three daies before.

We stood off all that night, and the next day being Wednesday; but the wind still continuing between the points of South-South-West, and West-South-West: so as we could not make any way to the Southward, in regard of our great want of water and wood (which was now spent) we much desired land and therefore sought for it, where the wind would best suffer vs to refresh our selues.

Thursday, the 16 of May, we stood in directly with the land, and much maruelled we descried it not, wherein we found our sea charts very false, putting land where none is.

Friday the 17 of May, about sixe a clocke at night we descried the land, which bare from vs North-North-East; but because it blew a great gale of winde, the sea very high and neere night, not fit to come vpon an vnknowen coast, we stood off till two a clocke in the morning, being Saturday: then standing in with it againe, we descried it by eight a clocke in the morning, bearing North-East from vs. It appeared a meane high land, *The description of the Iland.*

as

94   THE LAST DISCOVERY OF THE

as we after found it, being but an Iland[63] of some six miles in compasse, but I hope the most fortunate euer yet discoured. About twelue a clocke that day, we came to an anker on the North side of this Iland, about a league from the shore. About two a clocke our Captaine with twelue men rowed in his ship boat to the shore, where we made no long stay, but laded our boat with dry wood of olde trees vpon the shore side, and returned to our ship, where we rode that night.

63. The island was Monhegan, the most prominent landmark in approaching the coast. According to the Atlantic Coast Pilot, it is situated in Latitude 43° 46′ N., and in Longitude 69° 18′ W., and is distant from Thatcher's Island (Cape Ann) about 84 miles in a N. E. ½ E. course; from Seguin 19 miles on an E. course, and from Matinicus Light-houses about 20 miles on a W. by N. course. The island "lies N. E. and S. W. and is a mile and a half long, high, with steeply sloping shores, and quite bold to. Its northeastern end, called Green Point, is high and wooded; and a little to the southward of this, on the eastern face of the island, is a bluff, precipitous head, called Black Head. Thence the surface gradually descends towards the southwestern end, which is low and thickly wooded, and is known as Lobster Point." The lighthouse, a grey stone tower This 36 feet high, is about in the middle of the island, on a summit 140 ft. high, and is visible from a vessel's deck, on a clear night, 19 miles. Close in with the western shore of the island, about 200 yards off, is a small island, bare of all vegetation except grass, called Manana Island. Between the northern end of Manana and the western face of Monhegan are two bare islets, which form, with Manana and Monhegan, a small harbor of refuge, called Monhegan Harbor. *Vide* Atlantic Coast Pilot, Sub-Div. 4, pp. 302, 303. Capt. John Smith, who, in April, 1614, was at Monhegan, says: (Description of New England, p. 16, Force, Historical Tracts, Vol. 2, Veazie Reprint, p. 40,) "Monhegan is a rounde high ile; and close by it Monania, betwixt which is a small harbor where we ride."

NORTH PART OF VIRGINIA.   95

This Iland is woody, grouen with Firre, Birch, Oke and Beech, as farre as we saw along the shore; and so likely to be within. On the verge grow Gooseberries, Strawberries, Wild pease, and Wild rose bushes. The water issued forth down the Rocky cliffes in many places: and much fowle of diuers kinds breed vpon the shore and rocks.

While we were at shore, our men aboord with a few hooks got aboue thirty great Cods and Hadocks, which gaue vs a taste of the great plenty of fish which we found afterward wheresoeuer we went vpon the coast.[64]

From hence[65] we might discerne the maine land from the West-South-West to the East-North-East, and a great way (as it then seemed, and as we after found it)

vp

---

64. "The coast aboundeth with such multitudes of Codd, that the inhabitants of New England doe dunge their grounds with Codd; and it is a commodity better than the golden mines of the Spanish Indies." New English Canaan, p. 59, Force, Historical Tracts, Vol. 2. "The abundance of Sea-Fish are almost beyond beleeuing, and sure I should scarce haue beleeved it except I had seen it with mine own Eyes." New England's Plantation, p. 8, Force, Historical Tracts, Vol. 1.

65. It has been claimed that by these words Rosier means from Mon-began; but as he has just referred to the return of the boat to the anchorage of the Archangel, and to the occupation of the sailors while the party were ashore, it seems most natural to suppose that he means from the position of the ship, a league north of the island.

66. These words are held by some to mean "barely see"; but the same words occur in the former part of the sentence where they certainly cannot have this meaning, and it is fair to infer that they have the same signification in the two places.

vp into the maine we might discerne[66] very high mountaines,[67] though the maine seemed but low land; which gaue

67. Capt. Williams, of the U. S. Revenue Service, who, in 1797, at the request of Dr. Belknap, examined the coast of Maine with reference to Waymouth's discoveries, identified these mountains with what he calls the "Penobscot Mountains," meaning what are now known as the Camden Mountains. This was the accepted view until John McKeen (Coll. Me. Hist. Society, Vol. 5, pp. 313, 314) advanced the opinion that they were the White and Blue Mountains. He says: "It was this day probably clear, and the White and Blue Mountains in Maine and New Hampshire were visible and might have been seen thirty miles further to the eastward, as we are informed by the declarations of old mariners." No other writer, so far as I am aware, has referred to the Blue Mountains in this connection. R. K. Sewall (Ancient Dominions, p. 59), adopted the view that the high mountains seen by Waymouth were the White Mountains. He says: "The text implies a distant inland prospect of mountain views, as landmarks, which *might* *be discerned* from the anchorage, under what is conceded to be Monhegan Island, though it is not positive that they could be fully seen, as they were only discerned, which implies dimness,

as well as distance, of vision; and the White Mountains, showing in their magnificent outlines, terminating the view in the horizon of the distant west, along the valley of the Androscoggin, would seem to answer the object of the narrator as well as the description he gives, which was, so to shade the locality of the exploration and discoveries as to lead foreign voyagers, who might follow, astray." Dr. Edward Ballard (Popham Memorial Volume, p. 303) adopted the same view, and it is still held by some others. But William Willis (Coll. Me. Hist. Society, Vol. 5, p. 346) adhered to the earlier view advanced by Capt. Williams. He says: "We place ourselves by the side of the ancient mariner, Waymouth, as he lies in the 'Gift of God' [the Archangel] on the northern shore of Monhegan, and :before us 'descerne the mayne land and very high mountains.' The land surely can be no other than the shore from Pemaquid to Owl's Head, and the mountains the Camden and other heights bordering the Penobscot Bay, which now, as then, lift their lofty heads in silent, solemn grandeur before us. The White Mountains lie far to the west, more than 120 miles distant, and can only be seen under favorable circum-

gaue vs a hope it would please God to direct vs to the discouerie of some good; although wee were driuen by winds

stances." Prince took the same view (Coll. Me. Hist. Society, Vol. 6, p. 294, He says: "If we place ourselves near Monhegan in clear weather, we shall be at no loss to discover that the 'very high mountains' referred to are no other than the Camden and Union Mountains, which show their lofty heads far inland. . . . They are the only conspicuous heights along the coast, and a noted landmark for mariners approaching the land, being visible long before the main land comes into view." Rev. David Cushman (Coll. Me. Hist. Society, Vol. 6, pp. 309, 310), Johnston (History of Bristol and Bremen, p. 31), Bancroft (History of the United States, Revised Ed., Vol. 1, pp. 81, 82,) and others adopt the same view. It seems to me the only view that is tenable. The White Mountains can be seen from Monhegan only in the very clearest weather, and therefore only occasionally. Capt. Deering, who in the steamer Lewiston for many years has sailed along the coast of Maine, between Portland and Machias, says he has never seen Mt. Washington from the waters north of Monhegan. Capt. Denison of the steamer City of Richmond, who also has had a long experience on the coast of Maine, bears the same testimony. It is not denied that in very clear weather Mt. Washington can be seen from Monhegan, and on rarest occasions from the waters between Monhegan and the George's Islands. I spent a few days on Monhegan in August, 1885. The days went by but Mt. Washington was not visible. In the night of the 14th there was an aurora, and the wind, that had been to the southward for two days, blew very fresh from the northward early the next morning. The sky was without a cloud, and thinking that if ever I was to see Mt. Washington from Monhegan the time had come, I rose about four o'clock and walked over to the northern part of the Island near the school house. The Camden Mountains were clearly and sharply defined against the horizon, "a great way vp into the maine." But scanning carefully the horizon to the west, I failed to discern the White Mountains. A fisherman, whom I met, told me they could be seen only at sunset: at least, he had never seen them at any other time. About half past six o'clock, Mr. Humphrey, the assistant light-keeper, who knew I had visited Monhegan for the purpose of obtaining a view of the White Mountains from that point, informed me that Mt. Washington had been visible all the morning. With Mr. G. N. Faught, of Boston, I at once ac-

winds farre from that place, whither (both by our direction and desire) we euer intended to shape the course of our voyage. The companied Mr. Humphrey to the summit of the hill on which the light house stands. We halted at the entrance of the light house enclosure, and Mr. Faught and myself scanned the horizon to the west and northwest; but neither of us saw Mt. Washington until its exact position was indicated by Mr. Humphrey. Then we saw a faint blue mountain summit a little to the westward of Pemaquid Point light house. Holding it in view we descended the slope in order to note the point at which it was lost to sight. Just below the school-house, and about sixty feet from the ocean level as I estimated, the mountain disappeared. It was at this point that Capt. Charles Edwards, of the U. S. Light House Service, as he informs me, lost sight of Mt. Washington a few years ago when he made a like test. Mr. Humphrey assured me that he had often made this test with a like result. But it has been seen at the shore. April 11, 1885, at 6:39 P. M., William Stanley, keeper of the light, who at my request was noting the appearances of Mt. Washington from Monhegan, "surprised at the seeming near approach of Mt. Washington never before seen so plain," after lighting the lamp, left the lantern in care of Mr. Humphrey and descending the hill to the water's edge had a view of Mt. Washington at that point, and called several of the neighbors to bear witness to this singular occurrence, of which the peculiar state of the atmosphere was undoubtedly the occasion. Mr. Stanley, Oct. 17, 1885, sent me the following record of the views he had of Mt. Washington from Sept. 6 to that date:

"Sunday, Sept. 6, saw Mt. Washington plain from the shore at 6 a. m.

"Thursday, 10th, from tower 3 p. m.

"Thursday, 17th, very plain from hill 6 p. m.

"Sunday, 20th, 10 a. m. and from 5 to 6.30 p. m. Could not see it from the shore. Lost sight half way from the school house to the shore.

"Friday, 25th, plain from tower 7 a. m. and 6.30 p. m.

"Friday, Oct. 9th, from 5 to 6 p. m.

"Sunday, 11th, very plain from tower 4 to 6 p. m. Not visible from shore.

"Friday, 16th, plain from tower 4 to 6 p. m."

Oct. 23, after receiving the above record, I wrote to Mr. Stanley, requesting him to continue his observa-

The next day being Whit-Sunday; because we rode too much open to the sea and windes, we weyed anker about

tions. Dec. 31, 1885, he sent me the following additional report, signed by himself and Frederic F. Humphrey, assistant keeper.

"Oct. 26th, from 3 to 5 p. m., Mt. Washington was seen from lighthouse hill.

"Oct. 31st, 4.30 p. m., plain from the shore.

"Nov. 1st, 4.20 p. m., from tower.

"Nov. 10th, 4.30 p. m., from school house.

"Nov. 20th, 4.40 p. m., from tower.

"Nov. 26th, 4.25 p. m., very near sea level.

"Nov. 27th, 4.30 p. m., from tower.

"Nov. 28th, 4 p. m., from school house.

"Dec. 4th, from 3 to 5 p. m., plain from tower.

"Dec. 11th, 3.30 p. m., plain from hill.

"Dec 25th, plain all day from tower. Lose sight half way from S. H. to shore.

"Dec. 26th, plain 8 a. m., also 3.30 p. m., from tower.

"Dec. 27th, from 8 a. m. to 5 p. m., plain from tower."

This record shows that from early in September, 1885, to January, 1886, the White Mountains were seen only once *all day* from Monhegan, and only three times from *the shore*, and only

occasionally, morning or evening, from the *hill* or *light-house tower*.

Hon. C. W. Goddard, of Portland, without any reference to the point here at issue, kept a memorandum of his observation of the White Mountains from Portland during the three months preceding Jan. 1, 1887. In a communication, which will be found in the Portland *Press* of Jan. 3, 1887, he says: "A memorandum kept during the past three months shows that the White Mountains have been clearly visible between 7 and 7.30 a. m., only seven times, Oct. 17th, 24th, 25th, 26th, Nov. 5th, 27th and Dec. 6th. During the same period, they have been dimly discernable eight times; in all, 15 times only in 92 mornings, or less than one morning out of six."

I left Monhegan for Boothbay soon after my own observation of Mt. Washington as noted above; and though I looked for Mt. Washington again and again between Monhegan and Ocean Point—sailing over the same course traced by Waymouth, according to McKeen and others—it was not visible. And yet it was one of the clearest days of the season, and if ever the White Mountains served as a landmark in these waters they should have done so on that day; for the United States Meteorological

about twelue a clocke, and came along to the other Ilands more adjoyning to the maine,[68] and in the rode directly with the mountaines, about three leagues from the first Iland where we had ankered.

When we came neere vnto them (sounding all along in a good depth) our Captaine manned his ship-boat and sent her before with Thomas Cam one of his Mates, whom

observer on Mt. Washington sent that day, Aug. 15, the following despatch to the associated press: "This has been a perfect day. Ships on the ocean off Portland have been easily distinguished." *Vide* Portland Argus, Aug. 17, 1885. But though I could not see Mt. Washington from the water level even under these favorable circumstances, as we sailed away from Monhegan Harbor, and for miles, the Camden Mountains were in full view, far up in the main, their summits distinctly outlined against the sky. They are the most notable feature of the coast line as seen from Monhegan, and certainly no mariner approaching the coast could fail to mark them, and no one giving a description of the coast could fail to mention them. This Rosier did, if the mountains to which he refers were the White Mountains. For the bearing of an addition to Rosier's "Relation" at this point, as found in Purchas, His Pilgrimmes, see note 43. Capt. John Smith, De-

scription of New England, p. 13, Force, Historical Tracts, Vol. 2, refers to " the very high mountains of Penobscot, against whose feet doth beat the Sea," and adds, " But ouer all the Land, Iles, or other impediments you may well see them sixteene or eighteene leagues from their situation."

68. It is natural to understand by these words the islands between the place of anchorage (a league north of Monhegan) and the main land. The St. George's Islands, sixteen in number, extending in a line nearly N. NE. and S. SW. for about five miles, answer to this description. They are " in the rode directly with" the Union and Camden Mountains. Williamson (Hist. of Me., 1, p. 61) says Monhegan lies nine miles southerly of the St. George's Islands. The southern end of the outermost, Allen's Island, according to the Coast Survey Chart, bears N. by E. ¼ E. from Monhegan Light-house, distant about five miles and a half. The distance given by Rosier is of course

View of Monhegan Island from Muscongus Bay, Light bearing S.W. by S. distant 3½ Miles

View of St. George's Group and the Camden Mountains from Monhegan Island

Sketched by H.J.B '63

NORTH PART OF VIRGINIA.

whom he knew to be of good experience, to sound a search betweene the Ilands for a place safe for our shippe to ride in; in the meane while we kept aloofe at sea, hauing giuen them in the boat a token to weffe in the ship, if he found a conuenient Harbour; which it pleased God to send vs, farre beyond our expectation, in a most safe birth defended from all windes, in an excellent depth of water for ships of any burthen, in six, seuen, eight, nine and ten fathoms vpon a clay oaze very tough.

We all with great joy praised God for his vnspeakable goodnesse, who had from so apparent danger deliuered vs, & directed vs vpon this day into so secure an Harbour: in remembrance whereof we named it Pentecost harbor,[69] we arriuing there that day out of our last Harbour

Whitsunday.

---

only an estimate, and it will be seen that throughout the "Relation" Rosier's distances are in excess of actual measurements. But this difficulty is much increased if by "the other Ilands" are meant the Damiscove Islands (McKeen, Me. Hist. Soc. Coll., Vol. 5, p. 314), that is, the group of islands off Boothbay, the nearest of which must be fourteen miles from Monhegan. Besides, no one on a vessel a league north of Monhegan could possibly speak of these islands as "more adjoyning to the maine," and they are certainly not "in the rode directly with" the White Mountains.

69. McKeen (Me. Hist. Soc. Coll., Vol. 5, p. 314,) says: "To a person well acquainted with the coast, the several inlets, the harbors, and islands, there cannot be the least shadow of doubt that this Pentecost Harbor is that afterwards called Townsend Harbor, now Boothbay." But Boothbay Harbor cannot be reached by running in, from Waymouth's anchorage three miles north of Monhegan, "to the other Ilands more adjoyning to the maine." Further, Boothbay Harbor is not a harbor formed by islands alone, as the narrative requires, but by the shores of the main land and the outlying

Harbor in England, from whence we set saile vpon Easterday.

About foure a clocke, after we were ankered and well mored our Captaine with halfe a dozen of our Company went

islands. The depth of water, too, in Boothbay Harbor, does not agree with the statement in the "Relation." The narrative also implies that the main land was at a distance. Evidently recognizing the difficulties in identifying Boothbay Harbor with Pentecost Harbor, Sewall (Ancient Dominions of Maine, p. 74), says that Waymouth anchored between Fisherman's Island and Squirrel Island, off Boothbay Harbor. He has since identified Fishermen's Island Harbor with Pentecost Harbor. But this harbor, like Boothbay Harbor, is not reached by sailing in from Waymouth's anchorage "to the other Ilands more adjoyning to the maine." No one, too, would speak of the waters between Fisherman's Island Harbor and Squirrel Island as "a most safe birth defended from all windes," while in reference to the other points of identification mentioned above—the depth of water and the position in relation to the main land—the facts do not correspond with the facts recorded by Rosier concerning Pentecost Harbor. This is true, also, with reference to Fisherman's Island Harbor. Moreover, other points of identification to be considered further on are no less decisive against this theory. On the other hand, St. George's Harbor answers fully the requirements of the narrative. From Waymouth's anchorage it can be reached by sailing in "to the other Ilands more adjoyning to the maine." It is a harbor formed by islands—Allen's, Burnt, Benner's and Davis—and has four entrances. The main land, as is implied in the "Relation," is at a distance. Moreover the depth of water in the harbor, as given by Rosier, corresponds with the figures on the coast survey chart. The least depth given near the shore is four fathoms; but in the harbor proper there are six, seven, eight and a half, nine, ten and eleven fathoms, and the bottom is marked "hard." On the southern side of Davis Island, and between it and Allen's and Benner's Islands, according to the Atlantic Coast Pilot, p. 303, "is good anchorage in from four to eleven fathoms." Other points of identification will be considered as they occur in the narrative.

NORTH PART OF VIRGINIA.

went on shore[70] to seeke fresh watering, and a conuenient place to set together a pinnesse, which we brought in pieces out of England; both which we found very fitting.

Vpon this Iland, as also vpon the former, we found (at out first comming to shore) where fire had beene made: and about the place were very great egge shelles bigger than goose egges, fish bones, and as we judged, the bones of some beast.

Here we espied Cranes stalking on the shore of a little Iland adjoyning[71]; where we after saw they vsed to breed. Cranes.

Whitsun-munday, the 20 day of May, very early in the morning, our Captaine caused the pieces of the pinnesse to be carried a shore, where while some were busied about her, others digged welles to receiue the fresh water, which we found issuing downe out of the land in many places. Heere I cannot omit (for foolish feare of imputation of flattery) the painfull industry of our

---

70. McKeen (Maine Hist. Soc. Coll., Vol. 5, p. 315,) does not attempt to identify the island upon which Waymouth landed and afterwards set up the "pinnesse." Sewall thinks it was Fisherman's Island. Allen's Island, one of the St. George group, answers all the requirements of the narrative.

71. Benner's Island is separated from Allen's Island by a passage about two hundred yards wide, with three and a half fathoms at low water. The island is about seven hundred yards long. Sewall thinks "the little island adjoining" was Ram Island, which adjoins Fisherman's Island.

our Captaine, who as at sea he is always most carefull and vigilant, so at land he refuseth no paines; but his labour was euer as much or rather more than any mans: which not only encourageth others with better content, but also effecteth much with great expedition.

In digging we found excellent clay[72] for bricke or tile.

The next day we finished a well of good and holesome cleere water in a great empty caske, which we left there. We cut yards, waste trees, and many necessaries for our ship, while our Carpenter and Cooper laboured to fit and furnish forth the shallop.

We fished.

This day our boat went out about a mile from our ship, and in small time with two or three hooks was fished sufficiently for our whole Company three dayes, with great Cod, Haddocke, and Thornebacke.[73]

Abundance of many good fishes.

And towards night we drew with a small net of twenty fathoms very nigh the shore: we got about thirty very good and great Lobsters,[74] many Rockfish, some Plaise,

---

72. Clay is found on Allen's Island near the harbor shore, and water can still be secured in the manner described in this paragraph.

73. "We take plentie of Scate and Thornbacke." New England's Plantations, p. 9. Force, Historical Tracts, Vol. 1.

74. "We take plentie .... of Lobsters, that the least Boy in the Plantation may both catch and eat what he will of them. For my owne part I was some cloyed with them, they were so great and fat, and luscious. I haue seene some my selfe that haue weighed 16 pound, but others haue had diuers time so great Lobsters as haue weighed 25 pounds, as they assured me." New England's Plantations, p. 9. Force, Historical Tracts, Vol. 1.

Plaise,⁷⁵ and other small fishes, and fishes called Lumpes,⁷⁶ verie pleasant to the taste: and we generally obserued, that all the fish, of what kinde soeuer we tooke, were well fed, fat, and sweet in taste."

Wednesday, the 22 of May, we felled and cut wood for our ships vse, cleansed and scoured our wels, and digged a plot of ground, wherein, amongst some garden seeds,

75. The flounder. "There are excellent Plaice and easily taken. They (at flowing water) do almost come ashore, so that one may stepp but halfe a foote deepe, and pick them vp on the sands." New English Canaan, p. 61. Force, Historical Tracts, Vol. 2.

76. So named from the clumsiness of its form. It sometimes weighs seven pounds, and its flesh is very fine at some seasons. It is still occasionally found in our waters.

77. In Wood's New England Prospect," p. 36, in connection with an account of the fish in New England waters, occurs the following list in verse:
"The king of waters, the Sea shouldering Whale,
The snuffing Grampus, with the oyly Seale,
The storme praesaging Porpus, Herring-Hogge,
Line shearing Sharke, the Catfish, and Sea Dogge,
The Scale-fenc'd Sturgeon, wry mouthed Hollibut,

The flounsing Sammon, Codfish, Greedigut:
Cole, Haddocke, Haicke, the Thornebacke, and the Scate,
Whose slimie out side makes him selde in date,
The stately Basse old Neptunes fleeting post,
That tides it out and in from Sea to Coast.
Comforting Herrings, and the bony Shad,
Big-bellied Alewives, Machrills richly clad
With Rainebow colours, th' Frostfish and the Smelt,
As good as ever Lady Gustus felt.
The spotted Lamprons, Eeles, the Lamperies,
That seek fresh water brookes with Argus eyes;
These waterie villagers with thousands more,
Doe passe and repasse neare the verdant shore."

Corne sowed. seeds, we sowed peaze and barley, which in sixteen dayes grew eight inches aboue ground; and so continued growing euery day halfe an inch, although this was but the crust of the ground, and much inferior to the mould we after found in the maine.[78]

Friday, the 24 of May, after we had made an end of cutting wood, and carying water aboord our shippe, with fourteene Shot and Pikes[79] we marched about and thorow part of two of the Ilands; the bigger of which we judged to be foure or fiue miles in compasse, and a mile broad.[80]

The profits and fruits which are naturally on these Ilands are these:

All

---

78. "I made a Garden vpon the top of a Rockie Ile in 43½, 4 leagues from the Main, in May, that grew so well, as it serued vs for sallets in Iune and Iuly." Capt. John Smith, Description of New England, p. 9. Force, Historical Tracts, Vol. 2.

79. The flint-lock was not invented until the middle of the 17th century. The matchlock, subsequently referred to as used by Waymouth, was a cumbersome weapon, fired by a match like a cannon. The Pilgrims brought with them matchlocks. Capt. Miles Standish, however, had a Snaphance, a Dutch gun, which struck fire with a flint, but had no cover to the pan, and was a clumsy arrangement superseded by the flint-lock.

80. If these islands belonged to the St. George's group, the larger was Allen's Island, and the other Burnt Island, the next largest of the group, half a mile to the eastward of Allen's Island. The latter, according to the Atlantic Local Coast Pilot, "is nearly a mile and a half long." Monhegan, which to Rosier appeared "some six miles in compass," is not so long as Allen's Island, though a little wider. McKeen (Maine Hist. Soc. Coll., Vol. 5, p. 315,) says: "The larger is supposed to be Cape Newagen, the lesser Squirrel Island."

All along the shore and some space within, where the wood hindereth not, grow plentifully
- Rasberries.
- Gooseberries.
- Strawberries.[81]
- Roses.
- Currants.
- Wild-Vines.
- Angelica.[82]

The fruits of the Ilands.

Within the Ilands growe wood of sundry sorts, some very great, and all tall:
- Birch.
- Beech.
- Ash.
- Maple.
- Spruce.
- Cherry-tree.
- Yew.
- Oke very great and good.
- Firre-tree, out of which

issueth Turpentine in so maruellous plenty, and so sweet, as our Chirurgeon and others affirmed they neuer saw so good in England. We pulled off much Gumme congealed on the outside of the barke, which smelled like Frankincense.

---

81. Strawberries were greatly relished by the early settlers of New England. The Pilgrims found on Cape Cod "great store" of them. Mourt's Relation, Dexter's Ed., p. 20. Roger Williams (Key in R. I. Hist. Coll., 1, 90.) says: "This Berry is the wonder of all fruits growing naturally in those parts: It is of Itselfe Excellent: so that one of the Chiefest Doctors of England was wont to say, that God could have made, but God never did make a better Berry. In some parts where the Natives have planted I have many times seen as many as would fill a good ship within a few miles compasse."

82. An umbelliferous plant, so called because of its supposed angelic virtues. One species, *A. sylvestris*, common in Britain, was formerly greatly prized for its supposed virtues.

incense. This would be a great benefit for making Tarre and Pitch.

We stayed the longer in this place, not only because of our good Harbour (which is an excellent comfort) but because euery day we did more and more discouer the pleasant fruitfulnesse; insomuch as many of our Companie wished themselues setled heere, not expecting any further hopes, or better discouery to be made.

Pearle.

Heere our men found abundance of great muscels among the rocks; and in some of them many small Pearls: and in one muscell (which we drew vp in our net) was found foureteene Pearles,[83] whereof one of prety bignesse and orient; in another aboue fiftie small Pearles; and if we had had a Drag, no doubt we had found some of great valew, seeing these did certainly shew, that heere they were bred: the shels all glittering with mother of Pearle.

A Crosse erected.

Wednesday, the 29 day, our shallop being now finished, and our Captaine and men furnished to depart with hir from the ship: we set vp a crosse[84] on the shore side vpon the rockes.

Thursday,

---

83. The Pilgrims, when they anchored in Cape Cod Harbor, "found great Mussles, and very fat and full of Sea pearle." Mourt's Relation, Dexter's Ed., pp. 4, 5.

84. This is the only cross Rosier mentions as set up by Waymouth, except the one which was set up on the bank of the river which was subsequently discovered; and Rosier states further on in the "Relation" that they saw no crosses that had

NORTH PART OF VIRGINIA.   109

Thursday, the 30 of May, about ten a clock afore noon, our Captaine with 13 men more, in the name of God, and with all our praiers for their prosperous discouerie, and safe returne, departed in the shallop: leauing the ship in a good harbour, which before I mentioned, well mored, and manned with 14 men.

This day, about fiue a clocke in the afternoone, we *The Saluages came first to vs.* in the shippe espied three Canoas comming towards vs, which went to the iland adjoining, where they went a shore, and very quickly had made a fire, about which they stood beholding our ship: to whom we made signes with our hands and hats, weffing vnto them to come vnto vs, because we had not scene any of the people yet. They sent one Canoa with three men, one of which, when they came neere vnto vs, spake in his language very lowd and very boldly: seeming as though he would know why we were there, and by pointing with his oare towards the sea, we conjectured he ment we should be gone. But when we shewed them kniues and their vse, by cutting of stickes and other trifles, as combs and glasses, they came close aboard our ship, as desirous to entertaine our friendship. To these we gaue such things as we perceiued they liked, when wee shewed them the vse:

---

been erected by others. The fact, therefore, that Gilbert, in 1607, found a cross on one of the islands of St. | George's Harbor, is very strongly in favor of the identification of Pentecost Harbor with St. George's Harbor.

vse: bracelets, rings, peacocke feathers, which they stucke in their haire, and Tabacco pipes. After their departure to their company on the shore; presently came foure other in another Canoa: to whom we gaue as to the former, vsing them with as much kindnes as we could.

Three sorts of colours of painting.

The shape of their body is very proportionable, they are wel countenanced, not very tal nor big, but in stature like to vs: they paint their bodies with blacke, their faces, some with red, some with blacke, and some with blew.[85]

Their clothing and buskins.

Their clothing is Beauers skins, or Deares skins, cast ouer them like a mantle, and hanging downe to their knees, made fast together vpon the shoulder with leather; some of them had sleeues, most had none; some had buskins of such leather sewed: they haue besides a peece of Beauers skin betweene their legs, made fast about their waste, to couer their priuities.[86]

They

---

85. "Most of them paint the face black and red. These colors they mix with oil made from the seed of the sun-flower, or with bear's fat or that of other animals." Voyages of Samuel De Champlain, Prince Soc. Ed., Vol. 3, p. 166.

86. Friday, March 16, 1621, Samoset suddenly appeared at Plymouth. The next Sunday he brought with him five other Indians. Mourt describing them says: "They had every man a Deeres skin on him, and the principall of them had a wild Cat skin, or such like on the one arme; they had most of them long hosen vp to their groynes, close made; and aboue their groynes to their wast another leather, they were altogether like the *Irish* trousers; they are of complexion like our English Gipseys, no haire or very little on

They suffer no haire to grow on their faces, but on their head very long and very blacke, which those that haue wiues, binde vp behinde with a leather string, in a long round knot.

They seemed all very ciuill and merrie: shewing tokens of much thankefulnesse, for those things we gaue them. We found them then (as after) a people of exceeding good inuention, quicke vnderstanding and readie capacitie.[87]

[87]. their faces, on their heads long haire to their shoulders, onely cut before, some trussed vp before with a feather, broad wise, like a fanne, another a fox tayle hanging out . . . . some of them had their faces painted black, from the fore head to the chin, foure or fiue fingers broad; others after other fashions, as they liked." Mourt's Relation, Dr. II. M. Dexter's Ed., pp. 87, 88. Morton, referring to Indian apparel, says: "The Indians in these parts do make their apparrell of the skinnes of severall sortes of beastes, and commonly of those that doe frequent those partes where they doe live; yet some of them, for variety, will have the skinnes of such beasts that frequent the partes of their neighbors, which they purchase of them by Commerce and Trade. These skinnes they convert into very good lether, making the same plume and soft. Some of these skinnes they dresse with the haire on, and some with the haire off, the hairy side in winter time they weare next their bodies, and in warme weather they wear the haire outwardes." Morton's New English Canaan, Prince Soc. Ed., 141, 142. Smith has a like description: "For their apparell they are sometimes covered with the skinnes of wild beasts, which in winter are dressed with the hayre, but in Summer without. The better sort use large mantels of Deare skins, not much differing in fashion from the Irish mantels. Some imbrodered with white beads, some with copper, others painted after their manner." True Travels, Vol. 1, p. 129.

87. "Take these *Indians* in their owne trimme and naturall disposition, and they be reported to be wise, lofty spirited, constant in friendship to one another, true in their promise, and more industrious than many others."

112   THE LAST DISCOVERY OF THE

Their boats.

Their Canoas are made without any iron, of the bark of a birch tree, strengthened within with ribs and hoops of wood, in so good fashion, with such excellent ingenious art, as they are able to beare seuen or eight persons, far exceeding any in the Indies.

One of their Canoas came not to vs, wherein we imagined their women were: of whom they are (as all Saluages) very jealous.

When I signed vnto them they should goe sleepe, because it was night, they vnderstood presently, and pointed that at the shore, right against our ship, they would stay all night: as they did.

The next morning very early, came one Canoa abord vs againe with three Saluages, whom we easily then enticed into our ship, and vnder the decke: where we gaue them porke, fish, bread and pease, all which they did eat; and this I noted, they would eat nothing raw, either fish or flesh. They maruelled much and much looked

vpon

Thus concerning the "Tarrenteenes," Wood's New England's Prospect, Prince Soc. Ed., p. 68. "These people are not (as some have thought) a dull, or slender witted people, but very ingenious and very subtile." New English Canaan, p. 31. Force, Historical Tracts, Vol. 2. "We haue found the *Indians* very faithful in their Covenant of Peace with vs: very louing and readie to pleasure vs: we often goe to them, and they come to vs . . . . we for our parts walke as peaceably and safely in the wood, as in the hie-wayes in England, we entertaine them familiarly in our houses, and they as friendly bestowing their Venison on vs." Mourt's Relation, Dexter's reprint, pp. 133, 135.

NORTH PART OF VIRGINIA. 113

vpon the making of our canne and kettle, so they did at a head-peece and at our guns, of which they are most fearefull, and would fall flat downe at the report of them. At their departure I signed vnto them, that if they would bring me such skins as they ware I would giue them kniues, and such things as I saw they most liked, which the chiefe of them promised to do by that time the Sunne should be beyond the middest of the firmament; this I did to bring them to an vnderstanding of exchange, and that they might conceiue the intent of our comming to them to be for no other end.

About 10 a clocke this day we descried our Shallop returning toward vs, which so soone as we espied, we certainly conjectured our Captaine had found some vnexpected harbour, further vp[88] towards the maine to bring the ship into, or some riuer; knowing his determination and resolution, not so suddenly else to make returne: which when they came neerer they expressed by shooting volleies of shot; and when they were come within

---

88. If the Archangel was at anchor in St. George's Harbor, and Waymouth was returning from the St. George's River, this expression is perfectly accurate. With reference to St. George's Harbor the main is "further vp." The expression would not be accurate, however, if Waymouth was returning from the Kennebec, by the back waters from Bath to Boothbay and the Archangel was anchored either in Boothbay Harbor, or in Fisherman's Island Harbor, to both of which the main is near. Nor would it be accurate if Waymouth descended the Kennebec to its mouth, and thence made his way to either of these harbors.

within Musket shot, they gaue vs a volley and haled vs, then we in the shippe gaue them a great peece and haled them.

Thus we welcomed them; who gladded vs exceedingly with their joifull relation of their happie discouerie, which shall appeare in the sequele. And we likewise gaue them cause of mutuall joy with vs, in discoursing of the kinde ciuility we found in a people, where we little expected any sparke of humanity.

Our Captaine had in this small time discouered vp a great riuer, trending alongst into the maine about forty miles.[89] The pleasantnesse whereof, with the safety of harbour for shipping, together with the fertility of ground and other fruits, which were generally by his whole company related, I omit, till I report of the whole discouery therein after performed. For by the breadth, depth and strong flood, imagining it to run far vp into the

---

89. This was an estimate and is excessive on any theory. The words of McKeen (Me. Hist. Soc. Coll., Vol. 5, p. 317,) are worthy of notice here: "In travelling in any unfrequented region, especially when the mind is occupied and deeply interested in objects and scenery around, we are naturally prone to make no account of distance: it may be exaggerated, or very much diminished. So in going up a river, with or against a strong current, we may very much overrate, or fall short, in the actual distance; the principal danger, however, is in the former. We have an instance in this same river [the Kennebec is here referred to]. Soon after Capt. Popham arrived at the mouth of the Sagadahoc river, on the 17th of August, he, with Capt. Gilbert, ' sailed up into the river near forty leagues,' and returned at night. This must be an error, and such errors are not uncommon."

the land, he with speed returned, intending to flanke his light horsman for arrowes, least it might happen that the further part of the riuer should be narrow, and by that meanes subject to the volley of Saluages on either side out of the woods.

Vntill his returne, our Captaine left on shoare where he landed in a path (which seemed to be frequented) a pipe, a brooch and a knife, thereby to know if the Saluages had recourse that way, because they could at that time see none of them, but they were taken away before our returne thither. *Trifles left on shore.*

I returne now to our Saluages, who according to their appointment about one a clocke, came with 4 Canoas to the shoare of the iland right ouer against vs, where they had lodged the last night, and sent one Canoa to vs with two of those Saluages, who had beene a bord, and another, who then seemed to haue command of them; for though we perceiued their willingnesse, yet he would not permit them to come abord; but he hauing viewed vs and our ship, signed that he would go to the rest of the company and returne againe. Presently after their departure it began to raine, and continued all that afternoone, so as they could not come to vs with their skins and furs, nor we go to them. But after an howre or there about, the three which had beene with vs before
came

came againe, whom we had to our fire and couered them with our gounes. Our Captaine bestowed a shirt vpon him, whom we thought to be their chiefe, who seemed neuer to haue seene any before; we gaue him a brooch to hang about his necke, a great knife, and lesser kniues to the two other, and to euery one of them a combe and glasse, the vse whereof we shewed them: whereat they laughed and tooke gladly; we victualled them, and gaue them aqua vitæ,[90] which they tasted, but would by no meanes drinke; our beueridge they liked well, we gaue them Sugar Candy, which after they had tasted they liked and desired more, and raisons which were giuen them; and some of euery thing they would reserue to carry to their company. Wherefore we pittying their being in the raine, and therefore not able to get themselues victuall (as we thought) we gaue them bread and fish.

The intent of our kind vsage of the Saluages. Thus because we found the land a place answereable to the intent of our discouery, viz. fit for any nation to inhabit, we vsed the people with as great kindnes as we could deuise, or found them capable of.

The

---

90. "*Aqua vitæ*, a sort of cordial Liquor formerly made of brewed Beer strongly hopp'd, well fermented; now [1730] it is commonly understood of Spirits, Geneva, and the like."—Bailey. Yet in Mourt's Relation, Dexter's reprint, p. 17, in a reference to the landing of a party from the Mayflower on Cape Cod, it is stated, "we brought neither Beere nor Water with vs, and our victuals was onely Bisket and Holland cheese, and a little Bottle of aquavite."

The next day, being Saturday and the first of June, *We traded with the Saluages.* I traded with the Saluages all the fore noone vpon the shore, where were eight and twenty of them: and because our ship rode nigh, we were but fiue or sixe: where for kniues, glasses, combes and other trifles to the valew of foure or fiue shillings, we had 40 good Beauers skins, Otters skins, Sables, and other small skins, which we knewe not how to call. Our trade being ended, many of them came abord vs, and did eat by our fire, and would be verie merrie and bold, in regard of our kinde vsage of them. Towards night our Captaine went on shore, to haue a draught with the Sein or Net. And we carried two of them with vs, who maruelled to see vs catch fish with a net. Most of that we caught we gaue them and their company. Then on the shore I learned the names of diuers things of them: and when they perceiued me to write them doune, they would of themselues, fetch fishes, and fruit bushes, and stand by me to see me write their names.

Our Captaine shewed them a strange thing which they woondred at. His sword and mine hauing beene touched with the Loadstone, tooke vp a knife, and held it fast when they plucked it away, made the knife turne, being laid on a blocke, and touching it with his sword, made that take vp a needle, whereat they much maruelled. This

This we did to cause them to imagine some great power in vs: and for that to loue and feare vs.

Their Bowes and Arrowes.

When we went on shore to trade with them, in one of their Canoas I saw their bowes and arrowes, which I tooke vp and drew an arrow in one of them, which I found to be of strength able to carry an arrow fiue or sixe score stronglie; and one of them tooke it and drew

Their Bowes.

as we draw our bowes, not like the Indians.[91] Their bow is made of Witch Hazell, and some of Beech in fashion much like our bowes, but they want nocks, onely a string of leather put through a hole at one end, and

Arrowes.

made fast with a knot at the other. Their arrowes are made of the same[92] wood, some of Ash, big and long, with three feathers tied on, and nocked very artificiallie: headed with the long shanke bone of a Deere, made very sharpe with two fangs in manner of a harping iron.[93]

They

---

91. For the following information I am indebted to Francis Parkman, Esq., of Boston : "The English long bow was held perpendicularly, the left arm at full stretch, and the right hand drawn back, in shooting, to the level of the right ear. The Indians, in drawing the bow, did not necessarily hold it perpendicularly, but often at a slant, and drew back the right hand, not to the level of the right ear, but to that of the shoulder, or sometimes below it. This, at least, was the mode of shooting, which, as I have myself observed, was, and in some measure still is, practised by the Indians of the Plains. The eastern Indians, there can be little doubt, handled their bows in a similar way."

92. In the copy of the " Relation" procured in England by Jared Sparks, and published in the Collections of the Mass. Hist. Soc., 3d series, Vol. 8, the following words are here omitted: "a knot at the other. Their arrowes are made of the same."

93. The Pilgrims in their first conflict with the Indians picked up eight-

NORTH PART OF VIRGINIA.   119

They haue likewise Darts, headed with like bone, one *Their Darts.* of which I darted among the rockes, and it brake not. These they vse very cunningly, to kill fish, fowle and beasts.

Our Captaine had two of them at supper with vs in his cabbin to see their demeanure, and had them in presence at seruice: who behaued themselues very ciuilly, neither laughing nor talking all the time, and at supper fed not like men of rude education, neither would they eat or drinke more than seemed to content nature; they desired pease to carry a shore to their women, which we gaue them, with fish and bread, and lent them pewter dishes, which they carefully brought againe.

In the evening another boat came to them on the shore, and because they had some Tabacco, which they *Tabacco excellent.* brought for their owne vse, the other came for vs, making signe what they had, and offered to carry some of vs in their boat, but foure or fiue of vs went with them in our owne boat: when we came on shore they gaue vs the best welcome they could, spreading fallow Deeres skins for vs to sit on the ground by their fire, and gaue vs of their Tabacco in our pipes, which was excellent, and

---

een arrows, which they sent to their friends in England. Some of these arrows were "headed with brass, others with Harts horne and others with Eagles clawes." Mourt's Relation, with notes by H. M. Dexter, D. D., p. 55.

and so generally commended of vs all to be as good as any we euer tooke, being the simple leafe without any composition, strong, and of sweet taste; they gaue us some to carry to our Captaine, whom they called our Bashabes; neither did they require any thing for it, but we would not receiue any thing from them without remuneration.

Heere we saw foure of their women, who stood behind them, as desirous to see vs, but not willing to be seene; for before, whensoeuer we came on shore, they retired into the woods, whether it were in regard of their owne naturall modestie, being couered only as the men with the foresaid Beauers skins, or by the commanding jealousy of their husbands, which we rather suspected, because it is an inclination much noted to be in Saluages; wherefore we would by no meanes seeme to take any speciall notice of them. They were very well fauoured in proportion of countenance, though coloured blacke, low of stature, and fat, bare headed as the men, wearing their haire long:[94] they had two little male

The description of their Women and Children.

---

[94] "The women and girls always wear their hair in one uniform style. They are dressed like men, except that they always have their robes girt about them, which extend down to the knee. They are not at all ashamed to expose the body from the middle up and from the knees down, unlike the men, the rest being always covered. . . . There is a moderate number of pleasing and pretty girls, in respect to figure, color and expression, all being in harmony." Voyages of Samuel De Champlain, Prince Soc. Ed., Vol. 3, pp. 166, 167.

NORTH PART OF VIRGINIA.

male children of a yeere and half old, as we judged, very fat and of good countenances, which they loue tenderly, all naked, except their legs, which were couered with thin leather buskins tewed, fastened with strops to a girdle about their waste, which they girde very streight, and is decked round about with little round peeces of red Copper; to these I gaue chaines and bracelets, glasses, and other trifles, which the Saluages seemed to accept in great kindness.

At our comming away, we would haue had those two that supped with vs, to go abord and sleepe, as they had promised; but it appeared their company would not suffer them. Whereat we might easily perceiue they were much greeued; but not long after our departure, they came with three more to our ship, signing to vs, that if one of our company would go lie on shore with them, they would stay with vs. Then Owen Griffin (one of the two we were to leaue in the Country, if we had thought it needfull or conuenient) went with them in their Canoa, and 3 of them staied aborde vs, whom our whole company very kindly vsed. Our Captaine saw their lodging prouided, and them lodged in an old saile vpon the Orlop; and because they much feared our dogs, they were tied vp whensoeuer any of them came abord vs.

Owen

Owen Griffin, which lay on the shore, reported vnto me their maner, and (as I may terme them) the ceremonies of their idolatry; which they performe thus. One among them (the eldest of the Company, as he judged) riseth right vp, the other sitting still, and looking about suddenly cried with a loud voice, Baugh, Waugh: then the women fall downe, and lie vpon the ground, and the men all together answering the same, fall a stamping round about the fire with both feet, as hard as they can, making the ground shake, with sundry out-cries, and change of voice and sound. Many take the fire-sticks and thrust them into the earth, and then rest awhile: of a sudden beginning as before, they continue so stamping, till the yonger sort fetched from the shore many stones, of which euery man tooke one, and first beat vpon them with their fire sticks, then with the stones beat the earth with all their strength. And in this maner (as he reported) they continued aboue two houres.

The ceremonies of ye Saluages in their idolatry.

After this ended, they which haue wiues take them apart, and withdraw themselues seuerally into the wood all night.

They lie with their wiues secretly.

The next morning, as soone as they saw the Sunne rise, they pointed to him to come with them to our shippe: and haueing receiued their men from vs, they came

came with fiue or sixe of their Canoas and Company houering about our ship; to whom (because it was the Sabbath day) I signed they should depart, and at the next Sun rising we would goe along with them to their houses; which they vnderstood (as we thought) and departed, some of their Canoas coursing about the Iland, and the other directly towards the maine.

This day, about fiue a clocke after noone, came three other Canoas from the maine, of which some had beene with vs before; and they came aboord vs, and brought vs Tabacco, which we tooke with them in their pipes, which were made of earth, very strong, blacke, and sweet, containing a great quantity: some Tabacco they gaue vnto our Captaine, and some to me, in very ciuill kind maner. We requited them with bread and peaze, which they caried to their Company on shore, seeming very thankefull. After supper they returned with their Canoa to fetch vs a shore to take Tabacco with them there: with whom six or seuen of vs went, and carried some trifles, if peradventure they had any trucke, among which I caried some few biskets, to try if they would exchange for them, seeing they so well liked to eat them. When we came at shore, they most kindly entertained vs, taking vs by the hands, as they had obserued we did to them aboord, in token of welcome, and brought vs to sit
doune

doune by their fire, where sat together thirteene of them. They filled their Tabacco pipe, which was then the short claw of a Lobster, which will hold ten of our pipes full, and we dranke[95] of their excellent Tabacco as much as we would with them; but we saw not any great quantity to trucke for; and it seemed they had not much left of old, for they spend a great quantity yeerely by their continuall drinking: and they would signe vnto vs, that it was growen yet but a foot aboue ground, and would be aboue a yard high, with a leafe as broad as both their hands. They often would (by pointing to one part of the maine eastward) signe vnto vs, that their Bashabes[96] (that

The dwelling of Bashabes is Eastward fro ye great Riuer.

95. "Drinking" tobacco seems to have been the term employed when the reference was to *smoking* it; Massasoit, when he met the English at Plymouth for the first time, is described as "differing from the rest of his followers only in a great chain of white bone beads about his neck, and at it, behind his neck, hangs a little bag of tobacco, which he drank, and gave vs to drink." Drake, Book of the Indians, p. 22, cites an entry in the Plymouth records in 1646 as follows: "Anthony Thatcher and George Pole were chosen a committee to draw up an order concerning disorderly drinking of tobacco."

96. This word Rosier evidently understood to be a title. So did Gorges, who (Briefe Narration, Me. Hist. Soc. Coll., Vol. 2, p. 61,) says: "That part of the country we first seated in, seemed to be monarchical, by the name and title of a Bashaba." Godfrey (Me. Hist. Soc. Coll., Vol. 7, p. 06,) cites Champlain's Voyages (see Prince Soc. Ed., Vol. 2, p. 45,) and Relations des Jesuits, 1, ch. 3, 8, to show that Bashaba was a name, not a title; and the testimony has this value, that both Champlain and the Jesuits had a personal acquaintance with the Indian monarch, while Rosier and Gorges did not. As to the place of his abode, we learn from Strachey (Me. Hist. Soc. Coll., 8, p. 303) that the Indians who visited the Popham colonists, "departed in their canoas for the river of Pamaquid, promising Capt. Gilbert

NORTH PART OF VIRGINIA.

(that is, their King) had great plenty of Furres, and much Tabacco. When we had sufficiently taken Tabacco with them, I shewed some of our trifles for trade; but they made signe that they had there nothing to exchange; for (as I after conceiued) they had beene fishing and fowling, and so came thither to lodge that night by vs: for when we were ready to come away, they shewed vs great cups made very wittily of barke, in forme almost square, full of a red berrie[97] about the bignesse of a bullis,[98] which they did eat, and gaue vs by handfuls; of which

A red berrie which they feede on.

---

to accompany him in their canoas to the river of Penobscott, where the Bassaba dwells." Champlain, who sailed up the Penobscot in 1605 (Voyages, Prince Soc. Ed., Vol. 2, pp. 44, 45,) says: "I will drop this discussion to return to the savages who had conducted me to the falls of the river Norumbegue, who went to notify Bessabez, their chief, and other savages." These falls were evidently those a short distance above Bangor.

97. This could not have been the checkerberry, the taste of which is pleasant. The reference, probably, is to the partridge berry (*Mitchella repens*) which is found only in North and South America and Japan. "'The fruit is about the size of a whortleberry, broader than long, and being of two cohering ovaries shows the calyces of the two flowers; it is bright scarlet, and each half contains four bony nutlets in a white pulp. The berries remain on the plant through the winter, and it is not rare to find ripe fruit at the same time with the flowers in June. . . . The berries, while edible, are almost tasteless, and few care to eat them." Appleton's Cyclopædia, art. Partridge Berry.

98. The name of a round or spherical kind of plum, and is usually spelled now "bullace." In Polwhele's Glossary, "bullum" is stated to be a term used in Devon and Cornwall for "the wild plum, the bullace," and, with a similar meaning, is included in the East and West Cornwall Glossaries of the English Dialect Society, in Jago's Glossary of Cornwall, and in the Rev. H. Friend's Devonshire Plant Names. (Trans. Devon Asso., xiv., 1882, 540–1.) It is remarkable for being entirely, or almost entirely, re-

of which (though I liked not the taste) yet I kept some, because I would by no meanes but accept their kindnesse. They shewed me likewise a great piece of fish, whereof I tasted, and it was fat like Porpoise; and another kinde of great scaly fish, broiled on the coales, much like white Salmon, which the Frenchmen calle Aloza,[99] for these they would haue had bread; which I refused, because in maner of exchange, I would always make the greatest esteeme I could of our commodities whatsoeuer; although they saw aboord our Captaine was liberall to giue them, to the end we might allure them to frequent vs. Then they shewed me foure yoong Goslings, for which they required foure biskets, but I offered them two; which they tooke and were well content.

<small>We had yong Goslings of the Saluages.</small>

At our departure they made signe, that if any of vs would stay there on shore, some of them would go lie aboord vs: at which motion two of our Company stayed with them, and three of the Saluages lodged with vs in maner as the night before.

<small>June 3.</small>

Early the next morning, being Munday the third of June, when they had brought our men aboord, they came about our ship, earnestly by signes desiring that we would go with them along to the maine, for that there

---

stricted to these two counties. *Vide* Western Antiquary, Jan., 1886, p. 175.

99. The American shad (*Alosa præstabilis*), which attains a length of about twenty inches, and varies in weight from two to six pounds.

NORTH PART OF VIRGINIA. 127

there they had Furres and Tabacco to traffique with vs. Wherefore our Captaine manned the light-horseman[100] with as many men as he could well, which were about fifteene with rowers and all; and we went along with them. Two of their Canoas they sent away before, and they which lay aboord vs all night, kept company with vs to direct vs.

This we noted as we went along, they in their Canoa with their oares, would at their will go ahead of vs and about vs, when we rowed with eight oares strong; such was their swiftnesse, by reason of the lightnesse and artificiall composition of their Canoa and oares. *Their Canoa outrowed vs.*

When we came neere the point[101] where we saw their fires,

---

100. A large boat without a deck; probably not unlike the wooden whale-boat.

101. Sewall (Ancient Dominions of Maine, p. 74,), who makes Fisherman's Island Harbor Pentecost Harbor, thinks the reference is to Liniken's Point. If this were the fact, there would have been no need of Indians to "direct" Waymouth and his companions thither. The place was near, and the smoke of their camp would have been a sufficient guide. But the impression given by the entire narrative is that the main was at a distance. Another fact is to be borne in mind. These Indians —as will appear further on—were Pemaquid Indians. The earliest settlement of the English at Pemaquid was on the eastern shore. On Smith's map, John's Town—the name by which Smith designated Pemaquid —is far up on this shore. J. Wingate Thornton (Me. Hist. Soc. Coll., Vol. 5, p. 183,) says: "There was a popular tradition in the year 1750, that John Pierce settled on the eastern shore of Pemaquid, at Broad Bay." John Brown, who purchased of Samoset a large tract of land at Pemaquid, is called in the deed "John Brown of New Harbor." I am inclined to believe that at least some of the Indians who visited Waymouth in Pentecost Harbor

fires, where they intended to land, and where they imagined some few of vs would come on shore with our merchandize, as we had accustomed before; when they had often numbered our men very diligently, they scoured away to their Company, not doubting we would haue followed them. But when we perceiued this, and knew not either their intents, or number of Saluages on the shore, our Captaine, after consultation, stood off, and wefted them to vs, determining that I should go on shore first to take a view of them and what they had to traffique: if he, whom at our first sight of them seemed to be of most respect among them, and being then in the Canoa, would stay as a pawne for me. When they came to vs (notwithstanding all our former courtesies) he vtterly refused; but would leaue a yoong Saluage: and for him our Captaine sent Griffin in their Canoa, while we lay hulling a little off. Griffin at his returne reported, thay had there assembled together, as he numbered them, two hundred eighty three Saluages, euery one his bowe and arrowes, with their dogges, and wolues which they keepe tame at command, and not anything to exchange at all; but would haue drawen vs further vp
into

283 Saluages.

lived on the eastern shore, probably at New Harbor, and that the "point" mentioned by Rosier is at the entrance of the harbor, two miles and a half NE. by N. of Pemaquid Lighthouse.

NORTH PART OF VIRGINIA.

into a little narrow nooke[102] of a riuer, for their Furres, as they pretended.

These things considered, we began to joyne them in the ranke of other Saluages, who haue beene by trauellers in most discoueries found very trecherous; neuer attempting mischiefe, vntill by some remisnesse, fit opportunity affordeth them certaine ability to execute the same. Wherefore after good advice taken, we determined so soone as we could to take some of them, least (being suspitious we had discouered their plots) they should absent themselues from vs.

Tuesday, the fourth of June, our men tooke Cod and Hadocke with hooks by our ship side, and Lobsters very great; which before we had not tried. *Fish in the Harbour.*

About eight a clocke this day we went on shore with our boats, to fetch aboord water and wood, our Captaine leauing

---

102. Dr. De Costa (Mass. Hist. Soc. Proceedings, Vol. 18, p. 101, note) remarks: "That this 'little nook of a river' was Pemaquid River appears from the fact that, as Strachey says, Waymouth discovered not only 'the most excellent and beneficiall river of Sagadehoc,' but 'that little one of Pemaquid.'" The mention by Rosier of "this little nooke of a riuer," however, can hardly be magnified into a discovery. He gives it no such prominence. In all probability, also, as has been shown in the preceding note, Waymouth was at this time on the eastern shore of Pemaquid, and so could not have discovered the river to which Dr. De Costa refers. Rosier's language seems to imply that the "little nooke of a riuer" was near if not in sight, and the creek at New Harbor, on the southern side, near the point at the entrance, would seem to meet all the demands of the narrative.

130 THE LAST DISCOVERY OF THE

leauing word with the Gunner in the shippe, by discharging a musket, to giue notice if they espied any Canoa comming; which they did about ten a clocke. He therefore being carefull they should be kindly entreated, requested me to go aboord, intending with dispatch to make what haste after he possibly could. When I came to the ship, there were two Canoas, and in either of them three Saluages, of whom two were below at the fire, the other staied in their Canoas about the ship; and because we could not entice them abord, we gaue them a Canne of pease and bread, which they carried to the shore to eat. But one of them brought backe our Canne presently and staid abord with the other two; for he being yoong, of a ready capacity, and one we most desired to bring with vs into England, had receiued exceeding kinde vsage at our hands, and was therefore much delighted in our company. When our Captaine was come, we consulted how to catch the other three at shore which we performed thus.

Our manner of taking the Saluages. We manned the light horseman with 7 or 8 men, one standing before carried our box of Marchandise, as we were woont when I went to traffique with them, and a platter of pease, which meat they loued: but before we were landed, one of them (being too suspitiously feareful of his owne good) withdrew himselfe into the wood.

wood. The other two met vs on the shore side, to receiue the pease, with whom we went vp the Cliffe to their fire and sate downe with them, and whiles we were discussing how to catch the third man who was gone, I opened the box, and shewed them trifles to exchange, thinking thereby to haue banisht feare from the other, and drawen him to returne: but when we could not, we vsed little delay, but suddenly laid hands vpon them. And it was as much as fiue or sixe of vs could doe to get them into the light horseman. For they were strong and so strong as our best hold was by their long haire on their heads; and we would haue beene very loath to haue done them any hurt, which of necessity we beene constrained to haue done if we had attempted them in a multitude, which we must and would, rather than haue wanted them, being a matter of great importance for the full accomplement of our voyage.

Thus we shipped fiue Saluages, two Canoas, with all their bowes and arrowes. *We caught fiue Saluages, two Canoas, and their bowes and arrowes.*

The next day we made an end of getting our wood aboord, and filled our empty caske with water.

Thursday, the 6 of June, we spent in bestowing the Canoas vpon the orlop safe from hurt, because they were subject to breaking, which our Captaine was careful to preuent.

Saturday,

Saturday the eight of June (our Captaine being desirous to finish all businesse about this harbour) very early in the morning, with the light horseman, coasted fiue or sixe leagues about the Ilands adjoining, and sounded all along wheresoeuer we went. He likewise diligently searched the mouth of the Harbour, and about the rocks[103] which shew themselues at all times, and are an excellent breach of the water, so as no Sea can come in to offend the Harbour. This he did to instruct himselfe, and thereby able to direct others that shall happen to come to this place. For euery where both neere the rocks, & in all soundings about the Ilands, we neuer found lesse water than foure and fiue fathoms, which was seldome; but seuen, eight, nine and ten fathoms is the continuall sounding by the shore. In some places much deeper vpon clay oaze or soft sand: so that if any bound for this place, should be either driuen or scanted with winds, he shall be able (with his directions) to recouer safely his harbour most securely in water enough by foure[104] seuerall passages, more than which I thinke no man of judgement will desire as necessarie.

Vpon

Sounded about the rocks and mouth of the Harbour.

---

103. Such rocks are the Dry Ledges between Allen's Island and Burnt Island. The depth of water around them, according to the Coast Survey chart, corresponds with the figures given by Rosier. On the side next Burnt Island the channel is three hundred yards wide.

104. St. George's Harbor has four entrances easily recognizable. First, there is the passage between Burnt Island and Allen's Island, by which

NORTH PART OF VIRGINIA.

Vpon one of the Ilands (because it had a pleasant sandy Coue for small barks to ride in) we landed, and found hard by the shore a pond[105] of fresh water, which flowed

A ponde of fresh water.

Waymouth seems to have entered, when he left his anchorage north of Monhegan. Then there is the passage between Allen's Island and Benner's Island. A third passage lies between Benner's Island and Davis' Island. The fourth and widest passage is that between Davis' Island and Burnt Island. In all of these passages there is water enough to enter safely. But Fisherman's Island Harbor cannot be said to have four entrances, nor would one thus speak of Boothbay Harbor. *Vide* Coast Survey chart.

105. Prince (Me. Hist. Soc. Coll., Vol. 6, p. 296,) identifies this pond with the pond near the hamlets on Monhegan. But this pond receives its supply of water from surface drainage, and is not "fed with a strong run." Sewall (Ancient Dominions of Maine, p. 74,) locates the pond on Squirrel Island, where "the swamps of Waymouth's 'pond of fresh water' still empties its rivulet into the sea." McKeen (Me. Hist. Soc. Coll., Vol. 5, p. 319,) bears even stronger testimony on this point. "It is a well-known fact," he says, "that this island is now called Squirrel Island, with its sandy cove and fresh water pond." A fresh water pond and a rivulet would add to the attractions of this charming summer resort; but if they ever formed a part of the natural features of the place, of which there is no indication whatever, they have now disappeared. De Costa (Mass. Hist. Soc. Proceedings, Vol. 18, p. 101, note,) says: "The pond of fresh water, which flowed over the 'banks,' fed 'by a strong run,' which Rosier says could be made to 'drive a mill,' is situated on Cape Newaggin, opposite Pemaquid River, and is indicated on one of the maps of the Coast Survey. It has been examined for the writer, and corresponds exactly with Rosier's description, proving that Waymouth had been on the spot. The pond still flows over into the sea." Cape Newaggin is not opposite Pemaquid river, or any part of Pemaquid Point, but is far away at the mouth of the Sheepscot. It has no pond, nor is there, according to the Coast Survey chart, a pond on the island of which it forms a part. Furthermore, a careful examination of the Coast Survey chart fails to bring to view a pond on any one of the islands near the Pemaquid River. There is quite a large pond of fresh water on Damariscove Island, but it is not "fed

flowed ouer the banks, somewhat ouer growen with little shrub trees, and searching vp in the Iland, we saw it fed with a strong run, which with small labour, and little time, might be made to driue a mill. In this Iland, as in the other, were spruce trees of excellent timber and height, able to mast ships of great burthen.

While we thus sounded from one place to another in so good deepes, our Captaine to make some triall of the fishing himselfe, caused a hook or two to be cast out at the mouth of the harbour, not aboue halfe a league from our ship, where in small time only, with the baitt which they cut from the fish and three hooks, we got fish enough for our whole Company (though now augmented) for three daies. Which I omit not to report, because it sheweth how great a profit the fishing would be, they being so plentifull, so great and so good, with such conueint drying as can be wished, neere at hand vpon the Rocks.

Great plenty of Cod fish.

This day, about one a clocke after noone, came from the Eastward[106] two Canoas abord vs, wherein was he that

---

with a strong run" or a run of any kind. So far as I am aware, the only fresh water pond fed in this way, on any of the islands between Metinic and Seguin, is found on the eastern side of Allen's Island, and is indicated on the Coast Survey chart.

106. It is stated farther on in this paragraph that they came from "the Basbabes," whose abode was on the Penobscot. Those who had previously visited the ship are not spoken of as coming from the eastward. It seems to be a fair inference that the direction from which these two canoes came is mentioned because it

NORTH PART OF VIRGINIA. 135

that refused to stay with vs for a pawne, and with him six other Saluages which we had not seene before, who had beautified themselues after their manner very gallantly, though their clothing was not differing from the former, yet they had newly painted their faces very deep, some all blacke, some red, with stripes of excellent blew ouer their vpper lips, nose and chin. One of them ware a kinde of Coronet about his head, made very cunningly, of a substance like stiffe haire coloured red, broad, and more than a handfull in depth, which we imagined to be some ensigne of his superioritie; for he so much esteemed it as he would not for anything exchange the same. Other ware the white feathered skins of some fowle, round about their head, jewels in their eares, and bracelets of little white round bone, fastened together vpon a leather string. These made not any shew that they had notice of the other before taken, but we vnderstood them by their speech and signes, that they came sent from the Bashabes, and that his desire was that we would bring vp our ship (which they call as their owne boats, a quiden[107]) to his house, being, as they pointed,

Their ornaments of gallantnesse.

vpon

was not the same as that from which the Indians previously had come. But if Waymouth was at anchor in Fisherman's Island Harbor or in Boothbay Harbor, the Indians who had previously visited the ship—it is conceded that they were Pemaquid Indians—must also have come from the east.

107. The word used by the Indian was *aquiden*, the Abnaki word for canoe, the initial letter being very

vpon the main towards the East, from whence they came, and that he would exchange with vs for Furres and Tabacco. But because our Company was but small, and now our desire was with speed to discouer vp the river, we let them vnderstand, that if their Bashabes would come to vs, he should be welcome, but we would not remoue to him. Which when they vnderstood (receiuing of vs bread and fish, and euery of them a knife) they departed; for we had then no will to stay them long abord, least they should discouer the other Saluages which we had stowed below.

We went vp with our ship into the Riuer. Tuesday, the 11 of June, we passed vp[108] into the riuer

naturally regarded by Rosier as the indefinite article. Aquiden is one of the examples of the Abnaki noun used by Rev. M. C. O'Brien in his paper on the "Grammatical Sketch of the Ancient Abnaki Outlined in the Dictionary of Fr. Sebastian Râle, S. J.," read at the meeting of the Maine Historical Society, at Portland, Dec. 23, 1882, and printed in Vol. ix., of the Society's Collections, p. 272.

108. These words accurately state the course of a vessel leaving St. George's Harbor, and passing up into the St. George's River. But if Waymouth, leaving Fisherman's Island Harbor, entered the Kennebec through Townsend Gut, Sheepscot Bay and the Sasanoa River, it seems impossible that Rosier should have made the record as he did. It would not be an easy matter for a stranger to reach the Kennebec in this devious way. The Atlantic Coast Pilot (Sub. Div. 4, p. 405,) in its description of the Sasanoa River, says: "It flows through a very eccentric, crooked and dangerous channel... In the narrowest part of the channel the tidal current attains the extraordinary velocity of thirteen nautical miles an hour. Many ledges and rocks obstruct the passage of this river, and it is not possible for strangers to attempt it without disaster." Rosier makes no mention of any such perils in Waymouth's passage up the river, nor by any stretch of the imagination could he have spoken of the waters through which the ves-

NORTH PART OF VIRGINIA. 137

riuer with our ship, about six and twenty miles. Of which I had rather not write, then by my relation to detract from the worthinesse thereof. For the Riuer, besides that it is subject by shipping to bring in all traffiques of Marchandise, a benefit alwaies accounted the richest treasury to any land: for which cause our Thames hath that due denomination, and France by her nauigable Riuers recciueth hir greatest wealth; yet this place of itselfe from God and nature affoordeth as much diuersitie of good commodities, as any reasonable man can wish, for present habitation and planting.

The first and chiefest thing required, is a bold coast and faire land to fall with; the next, a safe harbour for ships to ride in.

The first is a speciall attribute to this shore, being most

---

sel made its way as "the riuer." Champlain that same season sailed up the Sheepscot to Wiscasset, and thence by the waters of Back River entered the Sasanoa at Hockomock Bay. He says: "Beyond this cape [Hockomock Point,] we passed a very narrow waterfall, but only with great difficulty; for, although we had a favorable and fresh wind, and trimmed our sails to receive it as well as possible, in order to see whether we could not pass it in that way, we were obliged to attach a hawser to some trees on shore and all pull on it. In this way, by means of our own, together with the help of the wind, which was favorable to us, we succeeded in passing it." (Voyages, Prince Soc. Ed., Vol. 2, pp. 58, 59.) If, as McKeen (Me. Hist. Soc. Coll., Vol. 5. p. 317) and Ballard (Popham Mem. Vol., pp. 304, 305) suppose, Waymouth, leaving Boothbay Harbor, followed the coast the mouth of the Kennebec—called by the former Sagadahoc as far as Merrymeeting Bay—then ascended to the river, Rosier's language is equally inapplicable.

140 THE LAST DISCOVERY OF THE

Heere are made by nature most excellent places, as Docks to graue or Carine ships of all burthens; secured from all windes, which is such a necessary incomparable benefit, that in few places in England, or in any parts of Christendome, art, with great charges, can make the like.

The Land. Besides, the bordering land is a most rich neighbour trending all along on both sides, in an equall plaine, neither mountainous nor rocky, but verged with a greene bordure of grasse, doth make tender vnto the beholder of hir pleasant fertility, if by clensing away the woods she were conuerted into meadow.

The wood. The wood she beareth is not shrubbish fit only for fewell, but goodly tall Firre, Spruce, Birch, Beech, Oke, which in many places is not so thicke, but may with small labour be made feeding ground, being plentifull like the outward Ilands with fresh water, which streameth doune in many places.

As we passed with a gentle winde vp with our ship in this Riuer, any man may conceiue with what admiration we all consented in joy. Many of our Company who had beene trauellers in sundry countries, and in the most famous Riuers, yet affirmed them not comparable to this they now beheld. Some that were with Sir Walter Ralegh[112] in his voyage to Guiana, in the discouery of the

---

112. Ralegh, with five ships, sailed for Guiana in 1595, and having explored to a considerable extent the country about the Orinoco, he re-

NORTH PART OF VIRGINIA. 139

est, where you shall neuer haue vnder 4 and 5 fathoms water hard by the shore, but 6, 7, 8, 9, and ten fathoms all along, and on both sides euery halfe mile very gallant Coues, some able to conteine almost a hundred saile, where the ground is excellent soft oaze with a tough clay vnder for anker hold, and where ships may ly without either Cable or Anker, only mored to the shore with a Hauser."[110] The ground of oaze and clay.

It floweth by their judgement eighteen or twenty foot at high water."[111] What flowe of water.

Heere

---

110. These statements with reference to the breadth and depth of the river, also with reference to the character of its bottom and the boldness of its shores, are true of the St. George's River. Then, too, on either shore of the St. George's River—a notable feature of the river—are the many "very gallant Coues" of which Rosier speaks. Many of these have names, and on the Coast Survey chart of the St. George's River I find Deep Cove, Gay Cove, Turkey Cove, Maple Juice Cove, Otis Cove, Watts Cove, Cutler's Cove, Broad Cove and Hyler's Cove. Furthermore, the direction of the river as it "runneth vp into the main" is, as Rosier says, "toward the great mountaines." All the way up the St. George's River to Thomaston one has before him the Camden and Union Mountains. If, however, Waymouth passed through Townsend Gut, crossed Sheepscot Bay, and by the way of the Sasanoa River—that "eccentric, crooked and dangerous channel"—reached the Kennebec at Bath, these statements by Rosier are strangely inaccurate. If he ascended the Kennebec from its mouth, the description is entirely misleading. Capt. John Smith sailed up the Kennebec a few years later, and this is his record (Description of New England, Veazie reprint, p. 42.): "Along this Riuer 40 or 50 miles I saw nothing but great high Cliffes of barren Rocks ouergrowne with wood."

111. The reference is to the flowing of the tide. It was only a "judgement," but the judgment was an erroneous one on any theory. The mean rise and fall of the tide in the St. George's River is 9.4 feet.

140 THE LAST DISCOVERY OF THE

Heere are made by nature most excellent places, as Docks to graue or Carine ships of all burthens; secured from all windes, which is such a necessary incomparable benefit, that in few places in England, or in any parts of Christendome, art, with great charges, can make the like.

The Land. Besides, the bordering land is a most rich neighbour trending all along on both sides, in an equall plaine, neither mountainous nor rocky, but verged with a greene bordure of grasse, doth make tender vnto the beholder of hir pleasant fertility, if by clensing away the woods she were conuerted into meadow.

The wood. The wood she beareth is not shrubbish fit only for fewell, but goodly tall Firre, Spruce, Birch, Beech, Oke, which in many places is not so thicke, but may with small labour be made feeding ground, being plentifull like the outward Ilands with fresh water, which streameth doune in many places.

As we passed with a gentle winde vp with our ship in this Riuer, any man may conceiue with what admiration we all consented in joy. Many of our Company who had beene trauellers in sundry countries, and in the most famous Riuers, yet affirmed them not comparable to this they now beheld. Some that were with Sir Walter Ralegh[112] in his voyage to Guiana, in the discouery of the

---

112. Raleigh, with five ships, sailed for Guiana in 1595, and having explored to a considerable extent the country about the Orinoco, he re-

of the Riuer Orenoque, which echoed fame to the worlds eares, gaue reasons why it was not to be compared with this, which wanteth the dangers of many Shoales, and broken ground, wherewith that was incombred. Others before that notable Riuer in the West Indies called Rio Grande; some before the Riuer of Loyer, the Riuer Seine, and of Burdeaux in France, which, although they be great and goodly Riuers, yet it is no detraction from them to be accounted inferiour to this, which not only yeeldeth all the foresaid pleasant profits, but also appeared infallibly to vs free from all inconueniences.

This riuer preferred before the Orenoque: and why.

I will not prefer it before our riuer of Thames, because it is England's richest treasure; but we all did wish those excellent Harbours, good deeps in a continuall conuenient breadth and small tide gates, to be as well therein for our countries good, as we found thē here (beyond our hopes) in certaine, for those to whom it shall please God to grant this land for habitation; which if it had, with the other inseparable adherent commodities here to be found; then I would boldly affirme it to be the most rich, beautifull, large & secure harbouring riuer that the world affoordeth.

Wednesday, the twelfth of June, our Captaine manned

turned to England the same year. He published on his return a glowing account of this voyage, entitled "Discovery of the large, rich and beautiful Empire of Guiana."

manned his light-horseman with 17 men, and ranne vp from the ship riding"³ in the riuer vp to the codde"⁴ thereof, where we landed, leauing six to keepe the light-horseman till our returne. Ten of vs with our shot, and some armed, with a boy to carry powder and match, marched vp into the countrey towards the mountaines, which we descried at our first falling with the land."⁵ Vnto some of them the riuer brought vs so neere, as we judged our selues when we landed to haue beene within a league

113. Waymouth seems to have anchored the Archangel near the present ruins of Fort St. George, a few miles below Thomaston.

114. This is an Anglo Saxon word, meaning 1, a pillow or cushion; 2, a bag; 3, the neck of a net; 4, a pod; 5, a large seed-basket. See Hollowell's Dict. of Archaic and Provincial Words, 1, 262. It is conjectured by Willis, McKeen and others, that it means here a narrow bay or indentation into the land. Capt. John Foster Williams, who in 1797 examined the coast of Maine with reference to Waymouth's discoveries in 1605, in his report says: "The word 'codde' is not common, but I have often heard it, as 'vp in the codde of the bay,' meaning the bottom of the bay. I suppose what he calls 'the codde of the river' is a bay in the river." Such a bay is found at Thomaston, at the bend of the river near where the Knox mansion stood.

115. It is impossible to reconcile this statement with the theory that Waymouth ascended the Kennebec. When the party landed, the mountains they saw at their first arrival on the coast seemed to be less than a league distant; and they started for them, purposing to reach them and return that night to the ship. The White Mountains cannot be seen from the landing at Bath, or at any landing on the Kennebec, and if they could, as Prof. Johnston (History of Bristol, Bremen and Pemaquid) suggests, "who would think of making a journey to them on foot, and returning the same day?" for they are about one hundred miles distant. On the other hand, Rosier's language answers fully to the geographical features of the country back of Thomaston.

a league of them; but we marched vp about foure miles We marched vp into ye land about 4 miles. in the maine, and passed ouer three hilles: and because the weather was parching hot, and our men in their armour not able to trauel farre and returne that night to our ship, we resolued not to passe any further, being all very weary of so tedious and laboursom a trauell.

In this march we passed ouer very good ground, Good pasture. pleasant and fertile, fit for pasture, for the space of some three miles, hauing but little wood, and that Oke like stands left in our pastures in England, good and great, fit timber for any vse. Some small Birch, Hazle and Brake, which might in small time with few men be cleansed and made good arable land: but as it now is will feed cattell of all kindes with fodder enough for Summer and Winter. The soile is blacke, bearing sundry hearbs, grasse, and strawberries bigger than ours in England. In many places are lowe Thicks like our Copisses of small yoong wood. And surely it did all resemble a stately Parke, wherein appeare some old trees with high withered tops, and other flourishing with liuing greene boughs. Vpon the hilles grow notable high timber trees, masts for ships of 400 tun: and at the bottome of euery hill, a little run of fresh water; but the furthest and last we passed, ranne with a great streame able to driue a mill.

We

144　THE LAST DISCOVERY OF THE

Deere, Hares, Hogges.　We might see in some places where fallow-Deere and Hares had beene, and by the rooting of ground we supposed wilde Hogs had ranged there, but we could descrie no beast, because our noise still chased them from vs.

We were no sooner come aboord our light-horseman, returning towards our ship, but we espied a Canoa comming from the further part of the Cod of the riuer Eastward,"⁶ which hasted to vs; wherein, with two others, was he who refused to stay for a pawne: and his comming was very earnestly importing to haue one of our men to go lie on shore with their Bashabes (who was there on shore, as they signed) and then the next morning he would come to our ship with many Furres and Tabacco. This we perceiued to be only a meere deuice to get possession of any of our men, to ransome all those which we had taken, which their naturall policy could not so shadow, but we did easily discouer and preuent. These meanes were by this Saluage practised, because we had one of his kinsemen prisoner, as we judged by his most kinde vsage of him being aboord vs together.

Thursday, the 13 of June, by two a clocke in the morning

116. According to those who hold the St. George's River theory, the "Cod of the riuer Eastward" was what is now known as Mill River. This was the usual route of the Indians coming from the Penobscot. Prince (Rosier's Narrative, p. 34) says that this carrying place has been used by the Indians within his knowledge.

NORTH PART OF VIRGINIA.   145

morning (because our Captaine would take the helpe and *We set vp another crosse.*
aduantage of the tide) in the light-horseman with our
Company well prouided and furnished with armour and
shot both to defend and offend; we went from our ship
vp to that part of the riuer which trended westward into
the maine,[117] to search that: and we carried with vs a
Crosse,[118] to erect at that point, which (because it was
not daylight) we left on the shore vntill our returne
backe; when we set it vp in maner as the former. For
this (by the way) we diligently óbserued, that in no place,
either about the Ilands, or vp in the maine, or alongst
the riuer, we could discerne any token or signe, that
euer any Christian had been before; of which either by
cutting wood, digging for water, or setting vp Crosses
(a thing neuer omitted by any Christian trauellers) we
should haue perceiued some mention left.

But to returne to our riuer, further vp into which
we then rowed by estimation twenty miles, the beauty
and

---

117. At Thomaston the river takes just such a course as is here described. Making a right-angle, it extends westerly about two miles, and then turns northward. The river narrows where it trends westward.

118. Rev. David Cushman (Maine Hist. Soc. Coll., Vol. 6, p. 316,) thinks the cross was set up at the second bend in the river, about two miles above Thomaston. The narrative, however, clearly states that the cross was set up at "that part of the riuer which trended westward into the maine," accordingly at the present site of Thomaston, or on the point opposite (Watson's Point), as Prince (Maine Hist. Soc. Coll., Vol. 6, p. 302) suggests.

146 THE LAST DISCOVERY OF THE

<small>Conuenlency of transportation.</small> and goodnesse whereof I can not by relation sufficiently demonstrate. That which I can say in generall is this: What profit or pleasure soeuer is described and truly verified in the former part of the riuer, is wholly doubled in this; for the bredth and depth is such, that any ship drawing 17 or 18 foot water, might haue passed as farre as we went with our light-horsman, and by all our mens judgement much further, because we left it in so good depth and bredth; which is so much the more to be esteemed of greater woorth, by how much it trendeth further vp into the maine: for from the place of our ships riding in the Harbour at the entrance into the sound, to the furthest part we were in this riuer, by our estimation was not much lesse than threescore miles."[119]

From

119. The distance Waymouth passed "vp into the river" with his ship was "about six and twenty miles." By this Rosier means the distance in the river alone; for the distance rowed in the boat on the 13th was "by estimation twenty miles." This would make the total distance in the river about forty-six miles. But the distance from Pentecost Harbor to the farthest point reached in the river he makes "not much lesse than threescore miles." These estimates are excessive on any theory. Like Rosier's estimation of the tide in the river, which for any part of the coast from the Penobscot to the Kennebec was exaggerated one-half, these estimates as to distance are much too large. It is to be borne in mind, however, that the discovery awakened great enthusiasm in Waymouth and his associates. The greatest rivers in the world were not comparable to this in their excited state of mind; and Rosier's record of what they saw bears throughout evidence that he shared the enthusiasm of the rest. *Vide* also p 114, note 89.

From ech banke of this riuer are diuers branching streames into the maine, whereby is affoorded an vnspeakable profit by the conueniency of transportation from place to place, which in some countries is both chargeable; and not so fit, by cariages on maine, or horsebacke.

Heere we saw great store of fish, some great, leaping aboue water, which we judged to be Salmons. All along is an excellent mould of ground. The wood in most places, especially on the East side, very thinne, chiefly oke and some small yoong birch, bordering low vpon the riuer; all fit for medow and pasture ground: and in that space we went, we had on both sides the riuer many plaine plots of medow, some of three or foure acres, some of eight or nine: so as we judged in the whole to be betweene thirty and forty acres of good grasse, and where the armes run out into the Maine, there likewise went a space on both sides of cleere grasse, how far we know not, in many places we might see paths made to come downe to the watering. *Meddow and Grasse.*

The excellencie of this part of the Riuer, for his good breadth, depth, and fertile bordering ground, did so rauish vs all with variety of pleasantnesse, as we could not tell what to commend, but only admired; some compared it to the Riuer Seuerne, (but in a higher degree) and we
all

all concluded (as I verily thinke we might rightly) that we should neuer see the like Riuer in every degree equall, vntill it pleased God we beheld the same againe. For the farther we went, the more pleasing it was to euery man, alluring vs still with expectation of better, so as our men, although they had with great labour rowed long and eat nothing (for we carried with vs no victuall, but a little cheese and bread) yet they were so refreshed with the pleasant beholding thereof, and so loath to forsake it, as some of them affirmed, they would haue continued willingly with that onely fare and labour 2 daies; but the tide not suffering vs to make any longer stay (because we were to come backe with the tide) and our Captaine better knowing what was fit than we, and better what they in labour were able to endure, being verie loath to make any desperate hazard, where so little necessitie required, thought it best to make returne, because whither we had discouered was sufficient to conceiue that the Riuer ran very far into the land. For we passed six or seuen miles, altogether fresh water (whereof we all dranke) forced vp by the flowing of the Salt: which after a great while eb, where we left it, by breadth of channell and depth of water was likely to run by estimation of our whole company an unknowen way farther: the search whereof our Captaine

We were loath to leaue the Riuer.

NORTH PART OF VIRGINIA. 149

taine hath left till his returne, if it shall so please God to dispose of him and vs."[120]

For we hauing now by the direction of the omnipotent disposer of all good intents (far beyond the period of our hopes) fallen with so bold a coast, found so excellent and secure harbour, for as many Ships as any nation professing Christ is able to set forth to Sea, discouered a Riuer, which the All-creating God, with his most liberall hand, hath made aboue report notable with his foresaid blessings, bordered with a land, whose pleasant fertility bewraieth it selfe to be the garden of nature, wherein she only intended to delight hir selfe, hauing hitherto obscured it to any, except to a purblind generation, whose vnderstanding it hath pleased God so to darken, as they can neither discerne, vse, or rightly esteeme the vnualuable riches in middest whereof they live sensually content

120. As the tide the next day, June 14—see farther on—was falling at four o'clock in the morning, Waymouth leaving his vessel at two o'clock had the advantage of the tide only a short distance. According to the narrative, if he was in the George's River, he was at the bend of the river, where Thomaston is situated, before daylight. At the highest point in the river which he reached he found, at least before he set out to return, that it had been "a great while eb." If, therefore, he returned on that same tide, as Rosier leads us to infer—"the tide not suffering vs to make any longer stay,"—it could not have been later than ten o'clock in the forenoon, and was probably earlier, when the bow of the lighthorseman was turned down stream. Eaton (Annals of the Town of Warren, p. 15) thinks that Waymouth ascended the St. George's River as far as the present town of Warren. Ships of 1200 tons have been built at this point.

150   THE LAST DISCOVERY OF THE

content with the barke and outward rinds, as neither knowing the sweetnes of the inward marrow, nor acknowledging the Deity of the Almighty giuer: hauing I say thus far proceeded, and hauing some of the inhabitant nation (of best vnderstanding we saw among them) who (learning our language) may be able to giue vs further instruction, concerning all the premised particulars, as also of their gouernours, and gouernment, situation of townes, and what else shall be conuenient, which by no meanes otherwise we could by any obseruation of our selues learne in a long time: our Captaine now wholy intended his prouision for speedy returne. For although the time of yeere and our victuall were not so spent, but we could haue made a longer voyage, in searching farther and trading for very good commodities, yet as they The cause of our speedy returne. might haue beene much profitable, so (our company being small) much more preiudiciall to the whole state of our voyage, which we were most regardfull now not to hazard. For we supposing not a little present priuate profit, but a publique good, and true zeal of promulgating Gods holy Church, by planting Christianity, to be the sole intent of the Honourable setters foorth of this discouery; thought it generally most expedient, by our speedy returne, to giue the longer space of time to make prouision for so weighty an entirprise."[121]   Friday,

121. This purpose was expressed by the Pilgrims in the memorable | compact signed in the cabin of the Mayflower in Cape Cod Harbor:

Friday, the 14 day of June, early by foure a clocke in the morning, with the tide, our two boats, and a little helpe of the winde, we rowed downe to the riuers mouth[122] and there came to an anker about eleuen a clocke. *We ankered at the mouth of the Riuer.* Afterward our Captaine in the light-horseman searched the sounding all about the mouth and comming to the Riuer, for his certaine instruction of a perfect description.

The next day being Saturday, we wayed anker, and with a briese from the land, we sailed vp[123] to our watering place, and there stopped, went on shore and filled all our empty caske with fresh water.

Our " Haviug vndertaken for the glory of God, and advancement of the Christian faith and honour of our King and Countrey a Voyage to plant the first Colony in the Northerne parts of VIRGINIA, doe by these presents solemnly & mutually in the presence of God and one of another, covenant and combine our selves together into a civill body politike, for our better ordering and preservation, and furtherance of the ends aforesaid."

122. "The riuers mouth" was of course the mouth of the great river Waymouth had discovered According to the narrative the ship "passed with a gentle wind vp" the river. The inference from these words as well as from the context plainly is that the ship passed up from the mouth of the river. It was now "rowed downe to the riuers mouth." There seems to be no escape from the conclusion, therefore, that Waymouth returned to Pentecost Harbor by the way he came. If he entered the Kennebec by the way of Townsend Gut, Sheepscot Bay and the Sasanoa River, he returned that way, and was not at the mouth of the Kennebec. If he proceeded from Pentecost Harbor to the mouth of the Kennebec, and thence ascended the river, Rosier's narrative signally fails to indicate this fact.

123 As St George's Harbor is not "vp" from the mouth of the St. George's River it is claimed that this passage is fatal to the view that the river discovered by Waymouth

<small>Our Captain made his certaine obseruation.</small>

Our Captaine vpon the Rocke[124] in the middest of the harbour obserued the height, latitude, and variation exactly vpon his instruments.

    1 Astrolabe.   4 Crosse Staffe.
    2 Semisphere.   5 And an excellent compasse
    3 Ringe instrument.   made for the variation.[125]

The certainty whereof, together with the particularities of euery depth and sounding, as well at our falling with

---

was the St. George's River, and Pentecost Harbor St. George's Harbor. It must be noticed, however, that Waymouth with his ship entered the river which he had discovered in his shallop. When he returned to Pentecost Harbor, the fact is recorded by Rosier in these words: "We descried our Shallop returning toward vs, which so soon as we espied, we certainly conjectured our Captaine had found some vnexpected harbour, *further vp towards the maine.*" If the shallop had been *up* it was now coming *down.* So when Waymouth left Pentecost Harbor with his ship to ascend the river, Rosier says: "We passed *vp* into the river." As the river descended was the same as that ascended, it is evident that Rosier's language in this paragraph cannot be pressed.

124. An identification of this "Rocke" is attempted neither by McKeen nor by any other writer, so far as I have noticed. There is a small island in St George's Harbor, and a little to the eastward (*Vide* the chart) is Carey's Rock.

125. In Purchas IV., p. 1606, we have the following reading at this point in the narrative: "Our Captaine vpon the Rocke in the middest of the Harbour made his certaine obseruation by the Sunne, of the height, latitude, and variation exactly vpon all his Instruments: 1. Astrolabe. 2. Semisphere. 3. Ring-instrument. 4. Cross Staffe. 5. And an excellent Compas, made for the variation. The latitude he found to be 43 degrees 20. minutes, North. The variation, 11. degrees 15. minutes, *viz*, one point of the Compas Westward. And it is so much in *England* at *Limehouse* by *London* Eastward." St. George's Harbor is in latitude 43° 25′ 45″ Boothbay Harbor is in latitude 43° 50′ 45″; Fisherman's Island Harbor is in latitude 43° 48′.

NORTH PART OF VIRGINIA. 153

with the land, as in the discouery, and at our departure from the coast; I refer to his owne relation in the Map[126] of his Geographicall description, which for the benefit of others he intendeth most exactly to publish.

The temperature of the Climate (albeit a very im- *The temperature of the* portant matter) I had almost passed without mention- *Climate.* ing, because it affoorded to vs no great alteration from our disposition in England; somewhat hotter vp into the Maine, because it lieth open to the South; the aire so wholesome, as I suppose not any of vs found our selues at any time more healthfull, more able to labour, nor with better stomacks to such good fare, as we partly brought, and partly found.

Sunday, the 16 of June, the winde being faire, and because we had set out of England vpon a Sunday, made the Ilands vpon a Sunday, and as we doubt not (by Gods appointment) happily fell into our harbour vpon a Sunday; so now (beseeching him still with like prosperity to blesse our returne into England our countrey, and from thence with his good will and pleasure to hasten our next arriuall there) we waied Anker and quit the Land vpon a Sunday.

Tuesday, the 18 day, being not run aboue 30 leagues from land, and our Captaine for his certaine knowledge how

---

126. If Waymouth published this map no copy, so far as I can learn, has been preserved.

how to fall with the coast, hauing sounded euery watch, and from 40 fathoms had come into good deeping, to 70 and so to an hundred: this day the weather being faire, after the foure a clocke watch, when we supposed not to haue found ground so farre from land, and before sounded in about 100 fathoms, we had ground in 24 fathomes. Wherefore our sailes being downe, Thomas King, boatswaine, presently cast out a hooke, and before he judged it at ground, was fished and haled vp an exceeding great and well fed Cod: then there were cast out 3 or 4 more, and the fish were so plentifull and so great, as when our Captaine would haue set saile, we all desired him to suffer them to take fish a while, because we were so delighted to see them catch so great fish, so fast as the hooke came downe: some with playing with the hooke they tooke by the backe, and one of the Mates with two hookes at a lead at fiue draughts together haled vp tenne fishes; all were generally very great, some they measured to be fiue foot long, and three foot about.

A fishing banke.   This caused our Captaine not to maruell at the shoulding for he perceiued it was a fish banke, which (for our farewell from the land) it pleased God in continuance of his blessings to giue vs knowledge of: the abundant profit whereof should be alone sufficient cause

to

NORTH PART OF VIRGINIA. 155

to draw men againe, if there were no other good both in present certaine, and in hope probable to be discouered. To amplifie this with words, were to adde light to the Sunne: for euery one in the shippe could easily account this present commodity; much more than those of judgement, which knew what belonged to fishing, would warrant (by the helpe of God) in a short voyage with few good fishers to make a more profitable returne from hence than from New-found-land: the fish being so much greater, better fed, and abundant with traine;[127] of which some they desired, and did bring into England to bestow among their friends, and to testifie the true report.

After, we kept our course directly for England & with ordinary winds, and sometime calmes, vpon Sunday the 14 of July about six a clocke at night, we were

---

127. Thomas Morton, in the "New English Canaan," published in 1632, in a chapter on the fishes that abound on the coast of New England, refers first of all to the "Codd, because it is the most commodious of all fish," and says "greate store of train oyle is mayed of the livers of the Codd, and is a commodity that without question will enrich the inhabitants of New England quickly; and is therefore a principall commodity." Capt John Smith was on the coast of Maine in 1614 and obtained "40,000 of drie fish, . . traine oile and Furres." New England's Trials, p. 10. John Winter, writing June 18, 1634, at Richmond's Island, to Robert Trelawny, says: "traine we haue made very little accordinge to our fish. All the winter fish doth yeld very little traine; we haue made but 5 hodgheds all this year." Trelawny Papers, p. 26. *Vide* also pp. 107, 162, 192, etc.

156 THE LAST DISCOVERY OF THE

We came into sounding. were come into sounding in our channell, but with darke weather and contrary winds, we were constrained to beat vp and downe till Tuesday the 16 of July, when by fiue a clocke in the morning we made Sylly[128]; from whence, hindered with calmes and small winds, vpon Thursday the 18 of July about foure a clocke after noone, we came into Dartmouth: which Hauen happily (with Gods gracious assistance) we made our last and first Harbour in England.

Further, I haue thought fit here to adde some things worthy to be regarded, which we haue observed from the Saluages since we tooke them.

First, although at the time when we surprised them, they made their best resistance, not knowing our purpose, nor what we were, nor how we meant to vse them; yet after perceiuing by their kinde vsage we intended them no harme, they haue neuer since seemed discontented with vs, but very tractable, louing, & willing by their best meanes to satisfie vs in any thing we demand of them, by words or signes for their vnderstanding: neither haue they at any time beene at the least discord among themselues;

---

128. The Scilly Islands, a group at the west entrance to the English channel. There are about one hundred and forty islands in all, besides numerous rocks. "The group was sometimes used by the Romans as a place of banishment, and was called by them Sellinæ or Silurum insulæ. They were annexed to the English crown in the 10th century." Appleton's Cyclopædia.

selues; insomuch as we haue not seene them angry but merry; and so kinde, as if you giue any thing to one of them, he will distribute part to euery one of the rest.

We haue brought them to vnderstand some English, and we vnderstand much of their language; so as we are able to aske them many things. And this we haue obserued, that if we shew them anything, and aske them if they haue it in their countrey, they will tell you if they haue it, and the vse of it, the difference from ours in bignesse, colour, or forme; but if they haue it not, be it a thing neuer so precious, they wil denie the knowledge of it.

They haue names for many starres, which they will shew in the firmament.

They shew great reuerence to their King, and are in great subiection to their Gouernors: and they will shew a great respect to any we tell them are our Commanders.

They shew the maner how they make bread of their Indian wheat, and how they make butter and cheese of the milke they haue of the Rain-Deere and Fallo-Deere, which they haue tame as we haue Cowes.

They haue excellent colours. And hauing seene our Indico, they make shew of it, or of some other like thing which maketh as good a blew. *Indico and other excellent colours in the countrey.*

One

One especiall thing is their maner of killing the Whale, which they call Powdawe;[129] and will describe his forme; how he bloweth vp the water; and that he is 12 fathoms long; and that they go in company of their King with a multitude of their boats, and strike him with a bone made in fashion of a harping iron fastened to a rope, which they make great and strong of the barke of trees, which they veare out after him; then all their boats come about him, and as he riseth aboue water, with their arrowes they shoot him to death; when they haue killed him & dragged him to shore, they call all their chiefe lords together, & sing a song of joy: and those chiefe lords, whom they call Sagamos, divide the spoile, and giue to euery man a share, which pieces so distributed they hang vp about their houses for prouision: and when they boile them, they blow off the fat, and put to their peaze, maiz, and other pulse, which they eat.

Their killing of the Whale.

129. Rev. M. C. O'Brien, of Bangor, who has made a special study of the Abnaki language, writes: "'Powdawe' means he blows, and describes the well known habit of the whale. *Pudébé* is the Abnaki for whale. *Pudébé pudawe* means the whale blows."

A Briefe Note of what Profits we saw the Country yeeld in the small time of our stay there.

TREES.
Oke of an exellent graine, strait, and great timber.
Elme.
Beech.
Birch, very tall & great; of whose barke they make their Canoas.
Wich-Hazell.
Hazell.
Alder.
Cherry-tree.
Ash.
Maple.
Yew.
Spruce.
Aspe.
Firre.
Many fruit trees, which we knew not.

FOWLES.
Eagles.
Hernshawes.
Cranes.
Ducks great.
Geese.
Swannes.
Penguins.
Crowes.
Sharks.
Rauens.
Mewes.
Turtle Doues.
Many birds of sundrie colours.
Many other fowls in flocks, vnknown.

BEASTS.
Reine-Deere.
Stagges.
Fallow-Deere.
Beares.
Wolues.
Beauer.
Otter.
Hare.
Cony.
Hedge-Hoggs.

160   THE LAST DISCOVERY OF THE

Polcats.
Wilde great Cats.
Dogges; some like Wolues,
   some like Spaniels.

FISHES.
Whales.
Seales.
Cod very great.
Haddocke great.
Herring great.
Plaise.
Thornebacke.
Rockefish.
Lobster great.
Crabs.
Muscles great, with pearles
   in them.
Cockles.
Wilks.
Cunner-fish.
Lumps.
Whiting.
Soales.
Tortoises.
Oisters.

FRVITS, PLANTS AND HERBS.

Tobacco, excellent sweet and strong.
Wild Vines.
Strawberries ⎫
Raspberries   ⎪
Gooseberries ⎬ abundance.
Hurtleberries ⎪
Currant trees ⎭
Rose-bushes.
Peaze.
Ground-nuts.
Angelica, a most soueraigne herbe.
An hearbe that spreadeth the ground & smelleth like Sweet Marioram, great plenty.
Very good Dies, which appeare by their painting; which they carrie with them in bladders.

The names of the fiue Saluages which we brought home into England, which are all yet alive, are these.

NORTH PART OF VIRGINIA.

1. Tahanedo, a Sagamo or Commander.
2. Amoret ⎫
3. Skicowaros ⎬ Gentlemen.
4. Maneddo ⎭
5. Saffacomoit, a seruant.[130]

[130]. The last of these names, Johnston (Popham Memorial, p. 294, note) says is a misprint for Sassacomoit, as the Abnaki Indians never used the letter f. Gorges (Briefe Narration, Me. Hist. Soc. Coll., Vol. 2, p. 17,) says that three of these Indians, on their arrival in England, came into his possession, and he gives their names as Manida, Skettwarroes and Tasquantum. The first two, it will be seen, are found in Rosier's list; but the last is the name of an Indian captured by Thomas Hunt, master of a vessel in Capt. John Smith's company in 1614, and through mistake is introduced here by Gorges' writing many years afterward. The capture of these Indians, Gorges (Me. Hist. Soc. Coll., Vol. 2, p. 17.) says, "must be acknowledged the means under God of putting on foot and giving life to all our plantations." From them Gorges learned "what goodly rivers, stately islands and safe harbors these parts abounded with . . . what great rivers ran up into the land, what men of note were seated on them, what power they were of, how allied, what enemies they had, and the like." Referring to the character of the three natives who came into his possession Gorges says: "After I had these people some time in my custody, I observed in them an inclination to follow the example of the better sort; and in all their carriages manifest shows of great civility far from the rudeness of our common people." It has been inferred from a remark by Gorges that the other two Indians brought over by Waymouth were assigned to Sir John Popham. In 1606 Gorges put two of the Indians, one of whom was Saffacomoit, on a vessel which he dispatched to America, under the command of Capt. Henry Challoung, with instructions to " keep the northerly gage, as high as Cape Britton, till they had discerned the main, and then to beat it up to the southward, as the coast tended, till they found by the natives they were near the place they were assigned to." But the Captain was taken sick, the course was not followed, and the vessel was captured by the Spaniards. Of the two savages, one at least, Saffacomoit, was subsequently recovered. A little later, the same season, and before the disaster that had befallen Capt. Challoung's expedition, another vessel, under Capt. Pring of Bristol, was sent out by Sir

John Popham, with instructions to follow and meet Challoung. Tahanedo, whom Gorges calls Dehamda—(Prof. Johnston, Popham Memorial, p. 293, note, says the native word was N'tahanada, and the change was on account of the English ear losing the first consonant and taking the second, or *vice versa*,—)and possibly Skicowaros, as Gorges intimates, accompanied Pring. Tahanedo was found at Pemaquid when the Popham Colony came over in 1607. If Skicowaros also accompanied Pring he must have returned to England, as he came over with the Popham Colony in the following year. After the colony had located at the mouth of the Kennebec Tahanedo visited the colony twice. We hear no more of him from that time until Capt. John Smith visited Pemaquid in 1614. Nor is he mentioned later. When eight or nine years after the visit of Smith, we again get a glimpse of affairs at Pemaquid, the names of Tahanedo and Skicowaros are no more heard,—all is changed and their places are filled by others (Johnston, Popham Memorial, p. 297.)

INDEX.

	Pages.
Abnaki Indians,	161
Advertiser, Portland Daily	72
Aix-la-Chapelle,	34
Albert, Archduke.	81
Aldworth, Robert	11, 47, 48
Allen's Island,	102, 103, 104, 106, 132, 133, 134
Aloza, (*Alosa praestabilis*)	126
Amidas, Philip	3
Amoret,	161
Anasou,	39, 40
Andros, Maj. Edmund	49
Androscoggin,	59, 66, 76, 96
Antiquaries, Society of	20
Aquiden,	135, 136
Archangel, The	viii, 142
Archer, Gabriel	8, 37
Arundell, Sir M.	14, 15
Arundell, Thomas	x, 14, 51, 81, 82
Astrolabe	25, 26
Atlantic Local Coast Pilot,	90, 91, 94, 102, 106, 136
Azores, The	89
Bache, Superintendent of Coast Survey,	69

	Pages.
Back River,	137
Bagaduce,	56
Ballard, Dr. Edward.	xi, 50, 61, 96, 137
Bancroft, George.	11, 67, 69, 70, 71, 72, 76, 97
Bangor,	125
Banks, Dr. C. E.	ix, 15
Barlow, Arthur	3
Bashabes,	124, 125, 134, 135, 136, 144
Bath,	ix, 59, 65, 67, 103, 139, 142
Baxter, James P.	vi, vii, 15, 20, 22, 33, 35
Belfast Bay,	56, 58, 64, 68
Belknap, Dr. J.	6, 7, 37, 54, 57, 64, 71, 75, 91, 96
Benner's Island,	102, 106, 132, 133
Beverly,	52, 75
Biencourt,	65
Birchwood, Sir George,	vii
Block Island,	54
Blue Mountains,	96
Boothbay Harbor,	ix, x, 58, 59, 61, 65, 67, 76, 99, 101, 102, 113, 133, 135, 137, 152.
Brereton, John,	8, 9, 31
British Museum,	22, 31, 33, 35, 71

INDEX.

Brown, John 127
Brown, John Nicholas............. v
Brown Library, John Carter....... v
Bryant, Hubbard W.............. xi
Bryce, Prof. James xi
Bullace,.................. 125
Burnham, John Milton........... v
Burnt Island, ... 102, 103, 133

Cabot, Sebastian................. 10
Calais,................. 86
Cam, Thomas............... 92, 100
Camden Hills, ix, x, 41, 63, 70, 96, 97, 100, 139
Cape Ann,.... 94
Cape Breton,.... .... 83, 161
Cape Cod,...... ....7, 39, 55, 68, 110
Cape Cod Harbor,................. 150
Cape Newagen,............. 100, 133
Capes of Virginia,.......... 52
Captain's Hill,.................... 11
Carey's Rock,.................... 152
Catherine, Queen,................ 14
Challoung, Capt. Henry 15, 83, 161, 162
Chamberlain, Ex-Gov. J. L........ 63
Champernown, Catherine.......... 1
Champlain,. 39, 43, 65, 71, 72, 73, 110, 120, 124, 125, 137
Charles II,.................... 48
Chesapeake Bay, ...4, 51, 52, 54
Coast Survey Office,................ x
Codde of the River,.........142, 144
Compass,................. 26
Connecticut River,.........53, 54, 75
Coves in St. George's River,· 139
Cross set up by Waymouth,. 108, 138, 146
Cuerno (Corvo)...... 80

Cushman, Rev. David....... 61, 69, 76, 97, 145
Cuttyhunk,....................... 7

Damariscove Islands, ... 101, 133
Dartmouth,............... 21, 55, 156
Davies, James............. 40, 49, 74
Davis Island,............... 102, 133
De Costa, Dr. B. F. 11, 40, 41, 42, 65, 66, 69, 70, 72, 73, 129, 133
Deering, Capt. Charles............ 97
Debanida,....................... 162
Demonstrations, Waymouth's,. 24, 25, 26, 28, 29, 31
Denison, Capt. W. E.............. 97
Deptford,........................ 33
Documentary History of Maine, 10, 13
Dover,........................ 86
Downs, The........ 86
Drake, Sir Francis,...... ....3, 4
Drake, Samuel A................. 62
Drake, Book of the Indians,. ...124
Dry Ledges,........ .... .132
Duke of York,............... 48, 49

Eaton........................... 61
East India Fellowship,.. vii, 16, 21, 82
Edgartown,....................... 11
Edward III...... 86
Edwards, Capt. Chas............. 98
Edwards, William S. xi
Elbridge, Giles.................... 47
Elizabeth, Queen..... 1, 2, 3, 4, 13, 16, 17, 20, 21, 30, 85.
Elizabeth Isle,................. 7, 45
Ellis, Sir Henry.................. 20
Emmanuel College, Cambridge,.. 33
Emperor of Cathay,........ 16, 17, 20

INDEX.

Essex,..........................13
Exeter,........................86
Falmouth, England.............6
Fish, Abundance of..95, 104, 147, 154
Fisherman's Island,............103
Fisherman's Island Harbor,...x, 102,
    127, 133, 135, 136, 152
Fishes, Names of..............100
Flint-lock gun,................106
Flores,........................89
Folsom, George.................58
Force, Hist. Tracts........94, 95, 100,
    104, 105, 106, 112
Fort Pownal,...................56
Fort St. George,...............142
Fortifications,................29
Fowles, Names of...............159
Friend, Rev. H.................125
Fruits, Names of...............100

Gilbert, Sir Humphrey........1, 2, 3
Gilbert, Otho..................1
Gilbert, Capt...40, 41, 42, 43, 44, 100,
    114, 124
Goddard, Hon. C. W.........viii, 99
Godfrey, J. F..................124
Goodwin Sands,.................86
Gorges, Sir Ferdinando...viii, ix, 15,
    41, 43, 45, 47, 50, 53, 74, 75,
    82, 83, 124, 161, 162
Gosnold, Bartholomew...6, 7, 8, 9, 10,
    11, 13, 21, 37, 43, 45, 51
Gravesend,.....................85
Gray, Prof. Asa................xi
Greenland,.....................20
Grenville, Sir Richard.........3
Griffen, Owen..........121, 122, 128
Griffith, William..............41

Guiana,....................140, 141
Hamlin, Prof. C. E.............87
Hanham, Thomas.................83
Hakluyt, Richard...............10
Harris, Dr. John...............viii
Hazard State Papers,...........3
Hockomock Bay,.............59, 137
Hockomock Point,...............137
Hogarth,.......................20
Holmes, Abiel,.................57
Howard, Edward.................14
Hubbard, Rev. William.......51, 75
Hudson's River,............52, 75
Humphrey, F. F.........97, 98, 99
Hunt, Thomas...................161
Indians captured by Waymouth..15,
    44, 71, 83, 130, 131, 161
Indians described by Rosier, ...109,
    110, 111, 112, 113, 115, 131, 156,
    157, 158.
Indians, Pemaquid..............40
Infanta Isabella Anne..........82

Jago's Glossary of Cornwall,...125
James I,......13, 22, 30, 33, 59, 81, 82
James River,...........52, 54, 75
Jamestown,.....................8
Jewell of Artes,........22, 23, 30, 31
John William, Duke.............34
John's Town,...................127
Johnston, Prof....62, 97, 142, 161, 162
Jülich, Siege of............34, 35

Kennebec,. ix, xi, 39, 40, 45, 49, 52, 57,
    59, 60, 61, 63, 65, 66, 70, 71, 72, 73, 74,
    75, 76, 113, 114, 136, 137, 139, 142,
    151.

INDEX

King's Library, ...22

Lane, Ralph 3, 4
Library of Lambeth Palace, ...40, 73
Light-horseman, ... .127
Liniken's Point, ...127
Lizards, The 87
Long Island, ...51, 52
Long Island, Penobscot Bay, ...56

Mace, Samuel 6
Mag. of Am. History, ...8, 11, 12, 69, 70, 72
Maine Hist. Soc. Coll. viii, 43, 46, 47, 48, 50, 58, 72, 83, 96, 101, 103, 106, 114, 124, 127, 133, 136, 137, 145, 161.
Manana, ... 94
Maneddo, ...161
Manomet, ...12
Martha's Vineyard, ...7, 11
Massachusetts Bay, ...7, 11, 53
Mass. Hist. Soc. Coll. v, 5, 8, 9, 37, 118
Mass. Hist. Soc. Proceedings, .. 41, 42, 129, 133, 138
Massasoit, ...124
Matchlock gun, ...106
Matinicus, ...41, 42, 94
Maurice, Prince 35
Maverick's Description of New England, ... 48
Mawooshen, ...47
Maximilian II., ...81
Mayflower, The 116, 150
McKeen, John ......58, 59, 60, 64, 69, 76, 96, 99, 101, 103, 106, 114, 133, 137, 142, 152.
Merrymeeting Bay, ...59, 66, 137
Metinic, ...42, 134

Milford Haven, ...10
Mill River, ...144
Mitchell, Henry 91
Monhegan, ...x, 40, 42, 46, 49, 55, 57, 62, 63, 64, 66, 68, 69, 70, 73, 74, 94, 96, 97, 98, 99, 100, 101, 103, 106, 133, 138.
Moosehead Lake, ...87
Morton's New English Canaan, ..111, 155.
Motley, J. L. 82
Mourt's Relation, .. 107, 108, 110, 111, 112, 116, 119
Muscovia and Turkey Companies, .. 82

Nahanada, ...44, 161
Nantucket, ...91
Nantucket Shoals, ...90
Narragansett, ...54, 75
Newagen, Cape. 106, 133
New England Hist. and Gen. Register, ...48, 65
Newfoundland, ...2, 5
New Harbor, ...44, 127, 128, 129
Northwest Passage to the Indies, ..vii, 16, 25
Norumbeague, ...125

O'Brien, Rev. M. C. 136, 158
Ocean Point, ...99
Old Fort Point, ...56
Oldmixon, ...50, 52, 54, 75
Oliver, Mrs. Hannah 12
Orinoco, ...140
Owl's Head, ...56, 96

Palfrey, J. G. 11, 60
Parkman, Francis 118

INDEX.   167

Partridge Berry,.................125
Partridge's Point,................44
Pejepscot,..... 59
Pemaquid,......42, 46, 49, 52, 73, 74,
75, 96, 127, 162
Pemaquid Harbor,................44
Pemaquid Indians,...........40, 135
Pemaquid Lighthouse,.. 128
Pemaquid Point,...........x, 44, 133
Pemaquid River,..ix, 43, 44, 47, 48, 50,
53, 129, 133
Penobscot Bay,.........10, 56, 58, 64
Penobscot Hills,.......55, 58, 96, 100
Penobscot River, ix, 41, 47, 57, 58, 59,
60, 63, 69, 71, 74, 76, 125, 134, 144
Pentecost Harbor,.ix, x, 43, 46, 53, 55,
57, 58, 59, 61, 62, 67, 72, 75, 76, 101,
102, 127, 151, 152.
Pentecost Harbor, Cross at......43,
108, 109, 138
Percy, George.....................8
Pette, Peter.... ... .33
Pette, Phineas................33, 34
Philipson, Miles.... 14
Pierce, John....................127
Pilgrims, The....... ....107, 108, 118
Pilgrims, Compact of the....150, 151
Platt, Master U. S. N............90
Plymouth,......................110
Plymouth Company,..............83
Plymouth Council,...............47
Plymouth Harbor,................11
Pole, George,...................124
Polwhele's Glossary, ...125
Popham, Capt. Geo........40, 59, 114
Popham Colony,.....40, 45, 46, 49, 65,
72, 73, 124, 128, 162
Popham, Sir John...14, 15, 45, 82, 83,
161, 162

Powhatan, River of.....51, 52, 54, 75
Prince, George. v, ix, 60, 62, 65, 69, 72,
76, 97, 133, 144
Prince, Thomas...............53, 75
Pring, Martin....8, 10, 11, 12, 13, 43,
44, 45, 83, 161, 162
Public Records Office,...........32
Purchas, his Pilgrimmes,...viii, 8, 37,
47, 49, 54, 74, 76, 100, 152

Quibiquesson,............ 47

Râle, Fr. Sebastian,..... 135
Raleigh, Carew................... 1
Raleigh, Sir Walter,...1, 2, 3, 4, 5, 6,
7, 10, 13, 14, 36, 37, 140
Raleigh, City of....................4
Ram Island,..... 103
Ratcliffe,............. 85
Resolution Island,................20
Revised Statutes of Maine,.......viii
Richmond's Island.. ..…........155
Roanoke Island,................3, 4
Rose and Crown Shoal,............91
Rosier, James.viii, ix, 31, 37, 38, 40, 43,
45, 46, 70, 73, 74, 76, 95, 100, 102,
106, 108, 124, 128, 129, 132, 133,
136, 137, 138, 139, 152, 161.
Royal Society,..................viii
Rudolph II,........ ....14, 81

Saffacomoit,................ 161
Sagadahock River,..ix, 45, 46, 48, 49,
53, 58, 59, 66, 71, 75, 114, 129, 151
Samoset,.......... ....110, 127
Sankaty Head,............... ...55, 91
Sasanoa River,..xi, 67, 136, 137, 139, 151
Sassafras,.............-........8, 11

INDEX

Savage Rock,.................7, 10
Scilly Islands,..................156
Seguin..... ....x, 42, 45, 134
Sewall, R. K....xi, 59, 67, 96, 102, 103,
127, 133
Sheepscot,.xi, 59, 65, 67, 133, 136, 137,
139, 151
Skidwarres (Skicowaros),.43, 44, 161,
162
Slafter,.........................40
Smith, Capt. John....8, 44, 46, 50, 73,
94, 100, 106, 127, 139, 155, 161, 162
Sparks, Jared................v, 118
Squirrel Island,........102, 106, 133
Standish, Capt. Miles............106
Stanley, William................98
St. Croix,...................48, 49
St. Croix, Island of..............39
Stepney,.......................86
Stevens, Henry,................vii
Stevens, Henry N........vii, viii
St. George's Harbor,.ix, x, 44, 55, 58,
61, 62, 67, 76, 102, 109
113, 132, 136, 152.
St. George's Island,....42, 44, 73, 138,
St. George's Islands,.......42. 55, 63,
68, 69, 70, 72, 73, 100, 103, 106
St. George's River,...x, 60, 61, 62, 65,
67, 68, 69, 70, 71, 74, 76, 113,
136, 139, 149, 151, 152.
Stith, Rev. William...........53, 75
St. James' Shells,..............87
Strachey, William.viii, ix, 3, 6, 14, 41,
46, 47, 49, 64, 71, 72, 74, 75, 124, 129

Tahanedo,..................161, 162
Tarbox, Rev. Increase N., D. D.,....2
Tarrenteenes,..................112

Tasquantum,..................161
Thames, The....................141
Thatcher, Anthony..............124
Thatcher's Island................94
Thayer, Rev. Henry O......42, 43, 72
Thirty Years War, Beginning of
the............................35
Thomaston,................142, 146
Thornton, J. Wingate............127
Tobacco,........123, 125, 127, 160
Tobacco, Drinking of............124
Townsend Gut,.....xi, 136, 139, 161
Townsend Harbor,.....58, 59, 101
Traine Oil,.....................155
Trees, Names of................159
Trelawny Papers,................155
Trelawny, Robert............ . .155
Two Bush Island, ...55, 56

Virginia,......................62

Virginia, Colonization of....3, 4, 5, 8
Warren, Town of 149
Warwick, Cape..................20
Waymouth, Capt. George } ..vi, vii,
Weymouth,   } viii, ix, x,
xi, 15, 16, 18, 19, 20, 21, 22, 25,
30, 31, 32, 33, 34, 35, 36, 39, 40,
43, 44, 45, 46, 47, 49, 50, 51, 52,
53, 54, 57, 58, 59, 60, 61, 62, 63, 64,
65, 67, 68, 69, 70, 71, 72, 73, 74, 75,
76, 82, 83; sails from Ratcliffe,
85; from Dartmouth Haven, 86;
reaches the Azores, 80; discovers
land, 91; amid shoals, 92; discovers an island, (Monhegan), 94;
description of the island, 95;
thence discerns the main and

INDEX.

high mountains up in the main, 96; sails in toward the other islands more adjoining to the main, 100; finds a good harbor, 101; and anchors, 102; finishes the shallop, 108; sets up a cross, 108; with thirteen men departs in the shallop, 109; the ship visited by Indians, 109; Waymouth returns with the shallop, 113; reports the discovery of a great river, 114; further intercourse with the Indians, 115-131; sounds about the rocks at the entrance of Pentecost Harbor, 132; discovers a pond of fresh water on one of the islands, 133; is visited by canoes from the Eastward, 134, 135; journey up into the river in his ship, 136, 137; profits of the river, 138; depth of the river and flow of tide, 139; comparison with other rivers, 140, 141; Waymouth leaves the ship and marches up into the country, 142, 143; returns to the ship, 144; sets up another cross, 145; distance in the river, 146; excellency of the river, 147, 148; extent of the discovery, 149; cause of the speedy return, 150; passes down to the river's mouth, 151; and thence to Pentecost Harbor, 152; sets sail for England, 153; on a fishing bank, 154; continues his course to England, 155; anchors in Dartmouth Haven, 156.

Western Antiquary,..............126
Westminster Abbey,.............10
White Head,........................x
White, John....................4, 6
White Mountains,...ix, 59, 66, 96, 97, 98, 99, 100, 101, 142
Whitson Bay,....................11
Whitson, John..................11
Williams, Capt. John Foster...54, 57, 64, 75, 91, 96, 142
Williams, Roger.................107
Williamson, Hon. Joseph........64
Williamson's Hist. of Maine,..48, 57, 67, 100
Willis, Hon. William...59, 68, 96, 142
Winter, John....................155
Wiscasset,......................137
Woods, Dr. Leonard,..........2, 13
Woods' New England Prospect,..105, 112
Woolwich,......................33
Wriothesley, Henry...6, 13, 14, 31, 51

The Gorges Society.

LIST OF MEMBERS, 1887.

Adams, Charles Francis	Boston.
Allen, Stillman Boyd	"
American Antiquarian Society,	Worcester.
Anderson, John Farwell	Portland.
Balcolm, George Lewis	Claremont, N. H.
Banks, Charles Edward	Chelsea, Mass.
Barrett, Franklin Ripley	Portland.
Barrett, George Potter	"
Baxter, Clinton Lewis	"
Baxter, Hartley Cone	"
Baxter, James Phinney	"
Bell, Charles Henry	Exeter, N. H.
Berry, Stephen	Portland.

Blake, Samuel Harward	Bangor, Me.
Blue, Archibald	Toronto.
Bonython, John Langdon	Adelaide, So. Australia.
Boston Atheneum,	Boston.
Boston Public Library,	"
Bowdoin College Library,	Brunswick, Me.
Bradbury, James Ware	Augusta, Me.
Briggs, Herbert Gerry	Portland.
Brown, Carroll	"
Brown, John Marshall	"
Brown, John Nicholas	Providence.
Brown, Philip Henry	Portland.
Brown, Philip Greely	"
Bryant, Hubbard Winslow	"
Burnham, Edward Payson	Saco, Me.
Burrage, Henry Sweetser	Portland.
Chicago Public Library,	Chicago.
Cleaves, Emery	Boston.
Cleaves, Nathaniel Porter	"
Colby University Library,	Waterville, Me.
Cole, Alfred	Buckfield, Me.
Conant, Frederic Odell	Portland.
Cutter, Abram Edmands	Boston.
Dana, Woodbury Storer	Portland.
Deane, Charles	Cambridge.
Deering, Henry	Portland.

LIST OF MEMBERS.

De Costa, Benjamin Franklin	New York.
Denham, Edward	New Bedford.
Dent, John Charles	Toronto.
DeWitt, John Evert	Portland.
Dexter, Henry Martyn	Boston.
Drummond, Josiah Hayden	Portland.
Dufossé, Edouard	Paris.
Elder, Janus Granville	Lewiston, Me.
Elwell, Edward Henry	Deering, Me.
Fessenden, Francis	Portland.
Field, Edward Mann	Bangor.
Fogg, John Samuel Hill	Boston.
Gerrish, Frederic Henry	Portland.
Goldsmid, Edmund	Edinburgh.
Hackett, Frank Warren	Portsmouth, N. H.
Hale, Clarence	Portland.
Hale, Eugene	Ellsworth, Me.
Hammond, George Warren	Boston.
Harris, Benjamin Foster	Portland.
Harvard University Library,	Cambridge, Mass.
Healy, James Augustine	Portland.
Hill, Winfield Scott	Augusta, Me.
Hyde, William Sage	Ware, Mass.
Jackson, George Edwin Bartol	Portland.
Jillson, Clark	Worcester, Mass.
Johnson, Edward	Belfast, Me.

Jordan, Fritz Hermann	Portland.
Jose, Horatio Nelson	Portland.
Lamb, George	Cambridge, Mass.
Lapham, William Berry	Augusta, Me.
Libby, Charles Freeman	Portland.
Library of Congress,	Washington.
Library of Parliament,	Ottawa.
Little, George Thomas	Brunswick, Me.
Littlefield, George Emery	Boston.
Locke, Ira Stephen	Portland.
Locke, Joseph Alvah	"
Maine Historical Society,	"
Maine State Library,	Augusta.
Maling, Henry Martyn	Portland.
Manning, Prentice Cheney	"
Manson, Alfred Small	Boston.
Massachusetts Hist. Society,	"
Massachusetts State Library,	"
Mosely, Edward Strong	Newburyport, Mass.
New Bedford Public Library,	New Bedford, Mass.
New England Historic Genealogical Society,	Boston.
New York State Library,	Albany, N. Y.
Noyes, Edward Alling	Portland.
Otis, Albert Boyd	Boston.
Paine, Nathaniel	Worcester, Mass.

LIST OF MEMBERS.

Pennsylvania Hist. Society,	Philadelphia.
Pierce, George J.	Boston.
Pierce, Josiah	London.
Poole, William Frederick	Chicago.
Portland Public Library,	Portland.
Pratt, John Frank	Chelsea, Mass.
Pullen, Stanley Thomas	Portland
Putnam, William LeBaron	"
Rand, George Doane	"
Reed, Thomas Brackett	"
Richardson, Charles Francis	Hanover, N. H.
Rich, Charles	Portland.
Scammon, John Young	Chicago.
Shapleigh, Waldron	New York.
Short, Leonard Orville	Portland.
Smith, Henry St. John	"
Soule, John Babson Lane	Highland Park, Ill.
Stearns, Charles Augustus	Boston.
Stevens, Henry Newton	London.
Stewart, George Jr.	Quebec.
Sweat, Lorenzo D. M.	Portland.
Symonds, Joseph White	"
Thomas, George Albert	"
Thompson, Joseph Porter	"
Trask, William Blake	Boston.
U. S. Dept. of State Library,	Washington, D. C.

GORGES SOCIETY.

Williamson, Joseph   Belfast, Me.
Woburn Public Library,   Woburn, Mass.
Woodbury, Charles Levi   Boston.
Woodman, Cyrus   Cambridge, Mass.
Woodward, James Otis   Albany, N. Y.
Worcester Free Public Library, Worcester, Mass.
Wright, William Henry Kearley, Plymouth, England.